THE TOTEM POLE

By the same author

Deep Play: A Climber's Odyssey from Llanberis to the Big Walls

THE TOTEM POLE

and a whole new adventure

PAUL PRITCHARD

ROBINSON
London

This paperback edition published 2000 by Robinson,
an imprint of Constable & Robinson Ltd
3 The Lanchesters
162 Fulham Palace Road
London W6 9ER

First published in Great Britain 1999
by Constable and Company Limited

ISBN 1–84119–243–0

Printed in the EU

A CIP catalogue record for this book
is available from the British Library

To all those who have suffered the horror
and confusion of traumatic brain injury and their families

Contents

LIST OF ILLUSTRATIONS

ACKNOWLEDGEMENTS

First must come my family: for putting you through this I am deeply sorry. Then I owe a debt of gratitude to Celia Bull for saving my life. I am eternally indebted to Neale Smith, Sergeant Paul Steane and Ian Kingston and his crew for executing the rescue so faultlessly and Andrew Davidson and Tom Jamieson for staying with me those long hours. My thanks go to Mr Van Gelder, Nicola Mackinnon, Dawn Lewis, Marge Conroy, Stormont Murray, Penny Croxford, Vera Simpson, Barbara Hartfall, Joy Hughes, Sian Hughes, Tricia Rogers, Jill Chappel, Lise Satherley and Fiona Parry for fixing me up so well; to Sue Duff for support and understanding; and to Jane Boucher for putting me right on a thing or two – I am grateful. There are too many nurses and helpers to mention here or even remember, but I thank you all.

My thanks to the film crew, Dave Cuthbertson, Mark Diggins, Meg Wicks, Richard Else, John Whittle, Brian Hall and Keith Partridge, who shepherded me back to the Totem Pole and to Steve Monks and Enga Lokey who climbed it for me. I am also indebted to Rod Staples for the loan of a boat.

I also owe my appreciation to Charlie Diamond, Gwion Hughes and George Smith for reading the script, to Maggie Body again for doing such an excellent job of editing the text. Karen Plas Coch, thank you for giving me the book on tarot cards, I am appreciative.

For the photographs a big 'cheers' to Simon Carter with thanks again going to Dawn Lewis, Brian Hall and Celia Bull. I am also grateful for the photographic inclusions of Sean Smith and the Royal Hobart Hospital. I must also thank Janet Smithies for her excellent ortwork on the cover. To Ben Lyon I am respectful of his unceasing patronage.

Finally my warm wishes to the patients (or clients) of Wirral Neurological Rehabilitation Unit.

Paul Pritchard
Llanberis, May 1999

Now I was free — morally free, as well as physically free — to make the long trek, the return, which still lay before me. Now the moral obscurity and darkness was lifted, as well as the physical darkness, the shadow, the scotoma. Now the road lay open before me into the land of light and life. Now, unimpeded, without conflict or blocks, I would run this good road, swifter and swifter, into a joy, a fullness and sweetness of life, such as I had forgotten or never known.

Oliver Sacks,
A Leg to Stand On

1

ICU

My eyelids fluttered open, leaving behind a greasy, blurry film obstructing my vision. All I could make out was a blinding white light shining on me, penetrating my being, or whatever was left of it. It wasn't my time to die. I knew it.

Marilyn Manson,
The Long Hard Road Out of Hell

It was about that time the staff nurse tried to kill me. It was so real that it is now etched on my conscious memory, like the engraving on a headstone, like it actually happened.

There was this very stocky nurse, who was of Malaysian origin. She had her hair balanced on top of her head in a bun, like black bread, and was wearing horn-rimmed spectacles. And then there were these six orthodox Jews. They had been visiting an old woman for a few days, presumably the mother of the woman who was married to the man.

And there was a little girl, too, with red hair and big blue eyes sitting on a sofa, obviously the daughter. She was wearing a blue dress and stared at me intensely, much more intensely than you would expect of a little girl. This strangely perturbed me and I remember thinking what piercing blue eyes she had. She was wearing white socks pulled up to her knees, her feet didn't reach the floor, and she seemed curiously ancient, ghostly in her appearance.

They decked out the old woman's bed in flowers and hid the

child in a cupboard. Then they had a funeral for the grandmother, there and then, while she was still alive, and they marched towards her bed singing 'Ave Maria'. She was moaning as if she was in great pain. There were six others with them now. The nurse, who was looking particularly fearsome, came last, syringe in hand. They stood around her, bouquets of roses and carnations all about them. The lethal injection was administered, slid through the skin in the crook of her elbow, and she drifted off into a peaceful and deathly slumber.

I was shrouded in a grey drizzle of horror. The old woman passed away without a word. I was a witness to murder. I curled up under the sheet and tried to make myself as small as I could or even invisible, which was impossible and I only succeeded in hiding my face. They all climbed into bunk beds and were each put to sleep by the same nurse. Not the long-term sleep that I feared, just diazepam deep.

Then they were all standing around me and I was sure I recognised their faces. I felt the same cold, lethal injection enter my jugular vein through the tube. I tried to fight off the terminal moment, but the pain falling from my body was too pleasant to resist. After fighting the drug for one . . . two . . . three . . . four . . . fi . . . seconds I drifted happily into oblivion.

It was difficult to recognise the moment when I came round. It could have been two minutes or two days ago. I didn't know where I was. Where was up? Where was down? Where were all these tubes and wires going? Up my nose. Into the jugular vein in my neck. Into the vein in my arm. Onto a peg on the end of my finger. Nurses kept coming over to my bed to administer drugs and I could feel their icy trickle flowing down my neck or up my arm. Then, as if by magic, my pain would disappear, would run off me like water and once again I would drown in a nice kind of way in that warm fluid.

The flexible plastic tube up my nose began choking me and my first thought was to get rid of all this stuff. I began ripping all the piping from out of my nose and arms and neck. I remember noticing that the tube in my nose just kept on coming, as if infinite in length, and was covered in a thin coating of yellow bile.

When the nurses came back around and saw what I had done they certainly weren't pleased. They told me off severely, I was scared, and then it was more painful having the tubes re-inserted afterwards. I had to swallow, gagging, as she pushed it up my nose, otherwise I felt the tube hitting the back of my teeth and saw it coming out of my mouth.

The first thing I remember was the induced darkness, like twilight, and the bleeping of the heart rate monitors. Then a male nurse came and sat by my bedside, wrapped the first joints of my fingers around a pencil and squeezed tight. He had an evil look on his face and seemed sinister to me. I only know he was squeezing the hell out of my fingers because I could see him. I could see his muscles flexing. I felt absolutely nothing. I tried to cry out but no sound came. I tried to pull my arm away but it would not move. It was heavy, leaden. He said something about shocking the system back into working. Anyway it didn't. A rising wave of panic swept through me. What was happening to me? Why was I here? Where was I anyway?

The whole ward was tilted in a rhomboid shape and all the beds and drip stands and trolleys tilted with it. And then I was falling and falling and spinning and spinning. Faster and faster. The bed was being spun around on its wheels at high speed and the next minute it was being rolled and tumbled. I held on tight with my hand and hooked my foot under the cot sides in fear that I was going to be pitched over the foot high guardrails on each side of the bed. I then vomited bile, cream in colour, over the clean white sheets.

I came around again and felt down below my waist with my left hand, as my right arm was like wood, there was no feeling in it at all. I felt down past my cock, which had a tube coming out of it as well, stretching it. I then felt lower down the bed. My left leg was intact, all the feeling of a normal leg and I could move it, too. Bend it at the knee and hip, pull my ankle up and drop it down again, wriggle my toes.

But where the hell was my right leg? I frantically felt around the mattress groping, unseen. I couldn't sit up to see what they'd done with my leg. A thousand thoughts ran through my head. They've amputated the fucker! Am I going to be in a wheelchair for the rest of my life or could I get by with a wooden leg? Images of me walking down the pavement on my prosthetic limb started to flash through my brain. *'What in fuck's name have you done with my leg!'* I screamed out silently to a passing nurse.

I intended to ring the bell but the plug came out of the wall and there was no way I could work out how to plug it in again. For an interminably long time I waited for the nurse to come and make everything better. But I knew she couldn't, this was my own private nightmare.

After an eternity the nurse came in and I tried asking her what she'd done with my leg, but nothing came out of my mouth. I tried the most powerful scream my lungs could muster. Still nothing. She walked straight past. Confused and bewildered, I couldn't work anything out.

Why do no words come out of my mouth? Not even an unintelligible sound. I became desperate. Then she came back and I beckoned to her frantically with my only functioning hand. I could tell she didn't understand, so I pointed to where my leg used to be. She threw the sheets back and gasped apologies.

She asked me how long my leg had been like that. I couldn't answer and anyway I didn't know what the hell she was on about. There was no leg there to be 'like that'. Then as if by some miracle my leg appeared again, now you don't see it, now you do. I was amazed. It had the appearance of someone else's leg. I didn't recognise it at all. In fact, I knew what it was; it was a corpse's leg. It was pallid, a deathly grey, like no other limb I ever saw. A funny looking splint on it made me think that I'd broken my leg. I couldn't care less.

I wept and wept and wept. I tried my damnedest to move my

4

leg but it wouldn't budge. There was no feeling in it and I couldn't tell where it lay. My arm was the same. No feeling in it at all and I didn't have a clue as to where it was. It felt like it wasn't there at all when I had my eyes shut and when I opened them again, and I could see where it was, it all became so obvious.

Then, all of a sudden, there was Celia's face, full of compassion and sorrow. She shed a tear and hid her face behind her hands. Again, I tried to speak. I wanted so much to comfort her. 'Don't worry. It's going to be all right. Just fine.' I hadn't a clue what had happened to me. I couldn't even remember the last place we had been. 'And by the way, I love you.'

Nothing came out. I began to panic as frustration set in. I couldn't even ask the nurse whether I would be like this for the rest of my life. It just seemed obvious at the time that this should be the first thing they tell you. It didn't register that they couldn't give me an answer. They just didn't know. And there was Celia not knowing either and wondering what kind of a vegetable she was going to have to live with for the rest of her life.

She left the room and came back with a piece of card with about twenty different pictures on it. The choice seemed bewildering at first. There were drawings of a dinner, a red cross, an ambulance, a needle, numbers from 0 to 9. I had double vision and the card seemed like a mosaic of tiny squares and patterns. I realised what I had to do. Eventually I managed to block off my right eye with my left hand and focus on the plastic laminated card for long enough to point to the symbol for house and the word PLEASE – Home, please.

With a lot of difficulty we developed some semblance of sign language. Thumb up meaning yes, thumb down meaning no, and a circle symbol joining thumb and index finger. Well, I never really grasped what that was supposed to indicate. That only confused me and, frustrated to hell, I would break down in tears. I would shake my head as furiously as it could be shaken, trying, without words, to explain about the nurse who tried to kill me. Celia would ultimately leave, to get a drink or something to eat, and I would be left with the nurse, who I was becoming significantly terrified of by now. She would prey around the foot of my bed and cackle.

Now I could no longer feel my left leg working, even though it was probably waving all over the place. I couldn't see it. Maybe it was the blurring of my vision, but I couldn't feel it either. So I perceived that I had nothing from the waist down. And of course my right arm didn't exist. I only had a sense of my left arm and my head. Abject horror gripped me as I lay with my left ear on the pillow, observing my one functioning limb. I pictured bloody entrails coming out from my waist, with organs, the pancreas and the liver, spilling out, tendons trailing out of my shoulder socket. I couldn't even sit up to look at myself because my legs weren't there and the weight was all to one side of my fulcrum. Like a torso with one arm I thrashed around under the sheet, utterly terrified. It reminded me of the movie where the guy gets sedated and wakes up with a leg missing, screams, the nurse sedates him again and when he wakes up next time another limb is missing, and so on.

We are now in the bottom of an infinitely tall, twilight-dark lift shaft and there are pipes and tubes rising all around us. We are swaying around, pitching and yawning like we're on a ship. Wait . . . I can hear the engine. We are on a ship! We can feel the vibration of a loud clanging, like an empty drum being hit with one of those mallets you see at strong man contests. Perhaps it's a crane lifting crates into the hull and banging them against it occasionally. And if you listen carefully, inside the din of the banging and engines and crates knocking together. If you put your ear to the side of the lift shaft, you can just make out a soft lapping of the waves. Like when your head's under water and you can hear the bubbles rising. And when you shout it sounds like someone else.

There's all these cables covered in thick black grease that start coiling around us. And another noise. Let's place it, shall we? It starts off high in pitch but then lowers and stops. Every time it stops we find more cables around us, until we can't even climb over them. The filthy black grease covers our hands and clothes but that's the least of our worries.

The ceiling is coming down towards us floor by floor, slowly, step by step, until it is right upon us. The floor of the lift, that is also the ceiling of the ward, crushes my right side and I can't escape. This is no dream, this is for real. You haven't got away so lightly. Your head is smashed in and your brain is oozing out.

Then I realise that I'm looking at myself and get mighty scared. Still the pitching and rolling and that noise of engines and clanging, and the ever more distant sound of the waves. I wait with you till dawn, which isn't really a dawn at all on the Intensive Care Unit, just a vague lightening through the curtains. And you evaporate, but the crushing of the lift remains, even though the room is back to its normal dimensions.

I thought I would be back to the mountains and crags in no time. It didn't occur to me then, it never had done, that I probably wouldn't go climbing again. Ever. I had built a life of rock climbing for myself. I was passionate about it. I had been a full-timer, living for the rock. I'd been all over the world with one motivation – climbing. Pakistan, India, South and North America, the Pamirs. I'd been to those places which dreams are made of. The midnight sun summit of Mount Asgard on Baffin Island, straddling the top of the slender pole that is Trango Tower in the Karakoram mountains, or with the puffins on the summit of the Old Man of Hoy in the Orkney Islands, looking down because all the world's below you, when everyone else is looking up. It didn't once occur to me that I might never climb again.

Celia is attempting to communicate with me. She is saying that I am in Tasmania, in the Royal Hobart Hospital, and that I was trying to climb the Totem Pole, on the Tasman Peninsula.

'You've been hit on the head by a rock and you have just gone through six hours' surgery.'

It doesn't make any sense. I understand the words but it just seems weird that I can be on the Tote one minute and then here, in hospital, with all these tubes coming out of me the next. I put my left hand to my head and have a feel around. It feels as though it's caked in congealed blood and it has loads of sticky tape on it. My hairstyle is like a monk's, bald on top but long on the sides and I can feel there's loads of blood matted into my hair, which makes it impossible to run my fingers through.

There's a huge squishy hole just left of the centre on my skull and I can feel metal staples through the tape. My neck hurts like hell. Any movement, an inch to the left or right leaves me in agony. At first I couldn't understand why, then it dawned on me that it must be the whiplash from the stone.

I remember the day now. Waking up in the tent, breakfasting on mangoes, bananas and oats and walking the eight kilometres out to the Totem Pole. I remember the Tyrolean rope traverse onto the Pole itself and rappelling down it.

There I hear the roaring of the waves like distant bombs exploding. I remember clipping the belay bolt at the end of the first pitch and carrying on down. There was a two-foot square dry piece of rock in all that turbulent swell; I can still smell the seaweed, like iron tastes.

I had no sooner got to it than I was up to my waist in the sea. Soaking wet. I shouted to Celia to come on down, but to stop at the ledge and tie the rope off there. At least we'd get a stab at the second pitch. I remember putting my rope ascenders on and making two moves on the rope before swinging to the left . . . Then nothing. I don't remember anything about the next fifteen minutes.

Then all the rest of it comes flooding back to me. Kinabalu, on the island of Borneo, the Malaysian Peninsula, Kuala Lumpur, Sydney, the Blue Mountains, Mount Buffalo, Melbourne and, finally, Tasmania. Our round the world trip. What had become of it? I was going to spend two months in the American desert, in Utah, two weeks of which Celia would be there with me. After that Dave Green was going to meet me and we were going to drive up the Alaskan Highway towards the Lightning Spur on Mount Thunder. Another summit that dreams are made of.

There. I see the Totem Pole. The void below the Tyrolean. Tying the knots in. Feet walking down the wall above the tossing swell. Aiming for that two-foot patch of dry rock. Taking the descender off and putting the clamps on.

The next moment I can remember I am shrugging my rucsac off into the sea. Celia is shouting at me, saying that I've got to help her if we're going to get out of this. I'm being held upright in slings, the grunting and laborious haul up, and now I'm getting dragged onto the ledge over that right-angled edge, making noises that sound nothing like me. I am realising for the first time that my right arm and leg aren't functioning.

In a state of delirium I began thinking that my pyjama trousers had all the makings of a fine shark-fin soup. I had all my things around me. Pots and pans, ladles and stirring spoons, a pot-bellied stove and a stack of firewood and the right ingredients. I managed to get my left trouser leg off but my leg brace was keeping my right one from coming off. And the fact that I couldn't move my leg meant that I had to resort to straining on tiptoes with my left to try and remove them. The catheter tube going down my trouser leg didn't help matters either. I rang the bell for assistance.

The nurse came in and I declared, 'Ark fin oup, yamas.' They were the first words I recall uttering. She pulled my trousers back up whilst, with some dismay, she asked the other nurse in a low voice what I'd been drinking. I seemed to be ringing that buzzer every five minutes on the ICU, asking other deluded and incomprehensible questions, the vast majority of which I've completely forgotten.

Then there was the time when a herd of Friesian cows walked past on the ceiling, which had turned from white, I think, to meadow green. There were lots of long shadows like trees close to sunset. And dry stone walls, stretching as far as eyes can see, in near perfect quadrangles. It was as if I was floating in a hot air balloon across farmland, looking down on the world from my airy basket.

It's now time for my bed bath. The hot towels feel wonderful down my whole left side. I do not feel any temperature down my right side, hot or cold. Now they flip me over and wipe my back down. I feel the cool draft on my back and, now, my front as they remove the towels. They fold me over as clean sheets are slid under me and over me. They fluff up my pillows and put new pillowcases on them. I have to lie on my back in here. It makes me feel clean and fresh to be out of those sweaty sheets, though my headache doesn't improve. It feels like a wild animal, a serval perhaps, trying to claw its way out of my head.

2

SUMMIT OF BORNEO

If you think you're something special in this world, engaging in a lofty inspection of the cosmos from a unique vantagepoint, your annihilation becomes unacceptable. But if you're really part of the great cosmic dance of Shiva, rather than a mere spectator, then your inevitable death should be seen as a joyous reunion with nature rather than as a tragedy.

V. S. Ramachandran
Phantoms in the Brain

I had to win the Boardman Tasker award with *Deep Play* if I was going to go on this round the world trip. It was the most prestigious award for mountain literature and my immediate future depended on it. The prize was a cheque for two thousand pounds and if I won I could visit a place I'd always dreamed of, Borneo. If I did win, and it was a big if, I would continue my trip to Australia, another country I'd always wanted to see, and then on to America. A grand for the air ticket and a grand spending money for six months sounded reasonable but I was up against the toughest opposition in the history of the award. And never before had six books been shortlisted.

As it included a Krakauer, a Simpson and a Perrin I surely didn't stand a chance. I could only hope that the judges, two of whom were big name alpinists, would, perhaps, be bored with reading books about Everest. It didn't occur to me to wonder why the Boardman Tasker Trust had invited me to bring a bunch of friends down to London from Llanberis. I thought that they just wanted

11

an injection of youth through the sober portals of the Alpine Club.

I took a team of the loudest girls you could imagine and as they laid into the sparkling white they only became louder. Peter Gillman's speech was unbearable. As chairman of the judges he dissected everyone's books and pulled mine apart the worst, saying that it had 'a banal first line'. The women made pistol-shooting impressions with their hands and he had to pause frequently to wait for them to quieten down.

Adrenaline was rushing through my arteries. It had only just occurred to me they would want to have the winning author present. Two shortlisted authors were North American and were not attending. It suddenly occurred to me, as I'm a bit slow on these matters, that there was only Joe Simpson and myself there of the six. I thought, ravenously excited, that it was a toss up between Joe and me.

I was already intoxicated and when the moment came I could hardly believe my ears. 'The winner of this year's Boardman Tasker award is . . . Paul Pritchard.' To the screams of my entourage I walked forward to collect my certificate and gave a very short speech because I was told to. 'Ta, I'm made up' was the extent of it. It turned out that Simon Yates' book, *Against the Wall*, about a trip he made with me to Patagonia was a very close second.

I posed for photos with my publishers. With Celia by my side I felt I had it all. We went crazy at a salsa club in Brixton, squirming and gyrating to the strains of the Lambada, rolling home in the daylight of early morning. And I knew that I was surely going on my round the world trip. Nothing could stand in our way now.

Celia surfaced from the wash. It was dawn and she was practising her dives off the jetty. Kinabalu was an ever-present entity that dominated the skyline like no other mountain I have seen. At sunrise, about 5.30 a.m., the mountain was silhouetted against reds and oranges, the shades of which you only witness on the equator.

We had decided to go snorkelling on the coral islands of Mamutik and Sapi before going on the mountain. We were a little stressed out by life at home and felt we needed a short holiday before committing ourselves to it. I'd never seen anything like the islands. Shoals of thousands of stripy fish, fish of all colours and sizes swam amidst equally brightly coloured coral. But it was far from paradise above the swell. An air compressor run by a generator put air in the divers' tanks. This was on all night and we couldn't get any sleep in our little tent. After two days we returned to the mainland exhausted.

We had found digs in Kota Kinabalu for fifteen ringets a night each, that's about two quid. Due to the economic crisis in Asia at that time the cost of living was very inexpensive for us but it meant all sorts of problems faced the Malaysians. Half-finished hotel blocks stood ghostly quiet in the hot afternoon sun. The tourist trade would have been booming were it not for the palls of smoke rising into the atmosphere from enormous forest fires in Kalimantan. We made a grand tour of the market places. Toads lurked in fish tanks with their eyes just above the waterline and crabs likewise; sea cucumbers, lobsters and eels were all alive. You could buy shark's fins and any manner of exotic fruit. The market places stretched for a good mile.

We bought a selection for our trip, packing the produce into two big hessian sacks – mangoes, melons, all sorts of vegetables, plastic bags of lentils and rice and beans, biscuits, savoury and sweet, bread, fat and suntan lotion. We only made a couple of mistakes, namely confusing some kind of fish dumpling for tofu. Then we loaded the stuff onto a bus and left the hot and sticky coast for the cool high villages of the Dusun, hair-pinning up and up through the deforestation towards Mount Kinabalu.

I sat next to a guy who worked for the Sultan of Brunei as an architect. He seemed to spend all his time building swimming pools and Jacuzzis for him. He explained to me about the traditional way of building houses on stilts here so that you get maximum air circulating and somewhere shady to work in the heat of the day. Brunei is the wealthiest country on earth and the Sultan even has Radio City, a London station, transmitted to apparently all his subjects.

There was a great waterfall up to the left that came off Kinabalu, and an open-topped wagon in front of the bus with a group of teenage boys in the back who kept slinging their empty beer cans into the road. This inflamed my anger until I noted that everyone was throwing cigarette packets and Coke cans out of the bus windows. This wild, tortuous road over the mountains was lined with refuse. But I soon became aware of the futility of my anger. I thought, it's no good preaching superficial tidiness when the West is responsible for the massive deforestation leading to the vast fires.

We passed a sign shaped like the mountain saying 'Welcome To Kinabalu National Park, Summit of Borneo'. There was a swish hotel and private chalets with restaurants and there was a bunkhouse, which is where we would stay. There were also miles of forest walks and a rainforest garden, which we paid to enter but, because we had no personal guide, it looked just the same as all the other forest. We tried to latch on to some Japanese tourists and listen to what their guide was saying, but he soon got wise and politely asked the tourists to make way for us. The line parted and we had to walk, slightly embarrassed, through.

We had dinner, a stir-fry, in one of the restaurants and I drank a glass of extra strength Guinness that tasted like gravy. I awoke in the dead of night feeling feverish. We arose at 5.30 a.m., packed and ate a hearty breakfast of cold greasy fried egg and beans, before boarding a bus to be shuttled the four miles up the steep climb to the start of the path. The first thing we saw was a sign of the record times for running up and down Kinabalu. 4 hours 34 minutes was the fastest time for the full 6560 feet of ascent all the way up to Low's Peak and then down again. It is a local Dusun lad who holds the record.

That day was hell for me. I would have given anything for it to end. Ahead was the biggest flight of steps I'd ever been asked to climb, 2000 metres of them, and here I was with a fever, feeling like I was going to pass out any time. Celia left me, at my insistence, and ran all the way to the summit. At least she was fit. She dumped her bag at the West Gurkha Hut and returned to the halfway hut, Gunting Lagadan, just as I was arriving.

Diary entry 31st December 1997

I am sitting in a hut halfway up Kinabalu, the Gunting Lagadan Hut (11,000 feet). I feel like shit. My nose is always blocked and I have terrible nights' sleep. My ears ache and my throat hurts. I must have picked something up snorkelling on those bloody coral islands. People have brought their guitars up and it looks like there will be New Year celebrations tonight.

We have hired three guys to help porter our stuff up the mountain and carried hefty packs ourselves. As we passed through the many altitude zones we discovered different forms of plant life. At about 8200 feet we got into pitcher plant territory. They're such outrageous plants they deserve some special mention. Picture a thin branch about the diameter of a bootlace and attach a litre container, a shapely vase, to the far end of it. Put a lid on it, hinged only at a narrow point. This is then used for drowning and digesting insects and small mammals.

Tomorrow we will watch the first sunrise of 1998 from the summit of Kinabalu. I can imagine it, being up there, the sun blinding us and casting long shadows. The shadows getting shorter as the heat of the sun intensifies. Her by my side.

As I lie here on the bed feeling grim, Celia is cranking, working hard carrying loads up to Sayat Sayat Hut with our two porters Spine and Jimmy. They earn 3 RM per kilo and carry 20 kilos to Sayat Sayat. They said 8 RM for a carry to the West Gurkha Hut, which is almost the same altitude but the other side of the plateau, so we decided on the Sayat Sayat option.

Spine is lithe with short-cropped, black hair, nylon flares and a colourful shirt with a massive collar. The skin on his face is dark yellow with a short nose dead centre; sizeable lips frame teeth as perfect as though they were made of porcelain. Apart from the hair he is the spit of Jimmy Hendrix. When we hired him he was just a few minutes off the record for running up and down Kinabalu. Jimmy was dressed similarly but with an even more colourful shirt, a flower pot hat and an absolutely trashed pair of trainers. He has the same look, typical of the Dusun, but a shocking set of teeth, like fence posts rotting in a muddy field.

We had been told by everybody that we would come up against a stone wall of bureaucracy if we said we wanted to climb on this mountain. Sam Lightner, in his article for the American *Climbing* magazine, stated that climbing was totally banned, ever since the British Army fiasco in Low's Gully. Najib Tahir, President of the Malaysian Alpine Club, told us we would be able to climb, as long as it wasn't anywhere near the Gully. Brian Hall, who was making a film about one of the soldiers who got lost in the Gully, said he had all sorts of problems getting permission to go down there. Robert New was the first person to descend it, all 13,125 feet of it to sea level. The Army, in their version of events, fail to mention this, but the less said about that episode the better.

So, we turned up and said, sheepishly, that we wanted to go climbing. We were sent to talk with the head of the park, James Liew, resplendent in full military dress and medals, who smiled at us and told us in a very friendly manner, 'No problem. Just a couple of formalities.' A form to be filled in and park insurance worth 3.50 RM – about fifty pence!

When we asked where we should meet our guide, because all trekkers must employ one, we were answered with another jovial question.

'Tell me, are you not experienced climbers?'

'Well . . . Yes.'

'Therefore you do not need a guide.'

Never once did he check our credentials. Our plan was to stay in the remote West Gurkha Hut for ten nights and climb around the plateau picking off several of its summits. In the perpetual fog which shrouds the mountain we wondered if we would be able to find this hut on the mile-broad plateau and we asked at the ranger station, 'Excuse me, do you have a map of Kinabalu?'

'Of course we do,' came the answer.

We were handed a very rough photocopy of a sketch that had no West Gurkha Hut marked on it at all.

'Where is the West Gurkha on here?' we asked in unison. 'Can you point to the position of where it is, even approximately?'

The ranger answered, 'Just follow the piles of stones down from the other side of the summit. There is no water at West Gurkha. Are you aware of this?'

That could present problems.

'We are taking bottles up,' we lied.

Well, I didn't see that sunrise from the summit of Kinabalu. I was dry retching. Celia came back that evening, having carried a load all the way to the Gurkha Hut. She was tired and not interested at the prospect of a 2 a.m. start to see the first dawn of the year. I had deteriorated and could barely get myself out of bed. We both awoke around midnight in our little dorm and wished each other happy new year, me grumpily. What a crap start to '98.

We breakfasted together and Celia left to carry loads from Sayat Sayat to West Gurkha. It started to rain torrentially. The waterfalls coming off the slabs opposite had to be seen to be believed, and it happened virtually the instant it started to rain. A wave of white water came over the top of the slab and then crashing down. If you happened to be climbing there when it started, God help you. There was such a roar from the weight of water, I found several trees washed down from up on the slabs. Celia later informed me that the rivers formed by the run off threatened to wash her into Low's Gully. I was really fretting.

She almost became lost on the plateau in a whiteout and when, soaked, she eventually found the hut, she couldn't get the key to work in the door. Eventually, crying with despair, she kicked the door and it unlocked. That night she slept alone up there, whilst

17

I sank into the depths of fever and misery in my six by six foot box. I wished I could be Superman for her but I failed at moments like this.

That night my epiglottis swelled up to the size of a slug, which I kept choking on, it was touching the back of my teeth, and I lapsed into delirium. 'Where is Celia?' I would mutter, thinking that she had forsaken me, though in reality I knew she was better off up on top of the mountain humping loads. 'Where is Celia?' . . . I dreamt back to Patagonia . . .

'There it is, the Shark's Fin.' That was the first time we had climbed alone together. A great dorsal blade of granite rearing up out of the French valley in a range of mountains called the Paine. We approached the mountain, coming up out of Antarctic beech forest and strolled across bouncy meadows of guanaco shrub with purple calafate berries scattered here and there. The silver threads of rivulets all had the same matrix, a distant glacier, but after only a short while dissipated as a premature delta before rejoining again to pour into the main artery.

We climbed without the rope for the first 800 feet but I felt increasingly worried should she fall. I knew this to be irrational because Celia wouldn't climb anything she might come off. She was always well in control. If she didn't feel that she was, then she'd back off or ask for a rope. We arrived at a ledge below a steep crack and made a joint decision to rope up. This crack was obviously the crux of the climb and I wanted her to lead it. It is the most gracious thing a mountaineer can do, offer your partner the hardest lead on the climb. I can hear her saying eagerly, 'I'll have a bash at it!'

She was up it in a flash, all knees and elbows, and we halted to survey the scene. We were poised on a knife-edge, slabs running convexly out of sight to our left and an overhanging 2000-foot wall to our right. A rock cornice, like an overhung deck of cards, projected a full ten feet out into space. We noticed this only when we went towards the edge on our hands and knees and found just a few inches of biscuity granite separating us from certain death. As we traversed the knife's edge we kept seeing summits which weren't summits at all, only false ones. And then there we were, standing together on the real summit, a block that looked like it could sheer off down the overhanging face at any moment. We looked around at the Fortress, the Cathedral, the Spade and the Leaf and we laughed and laughed and laughed . . .

. . . until I woke myself up.

In the heat of my fever my body became an engine with various organs hanging around my cell, my liver throbbing and my heart beating like there was no tomorrow. Pipes and pistons linked these. With each breath I could feel the hydraulic pump of my lungs, my arteries and veins were rubber hoses. My head was way out in the top corner of the cell looking down on everything. That was a long, long night.

Celia came again in the morning and she informed me of what a horror show she'd had with the lock. We cuddled for a while on the bed and then she went back up. It began raining again and I desperately hoped, after a third night, that I would make it up there tomorrow. Days were blending into nights into days again and my dreams had become absurd, usually frantic struggles against the wind or away from pursuers.

The hut has a cafe and hot showers but after six days it becomes a little wearing. We had no antibiotics; we'd forgotten them. The manager, a young lad who spoke no words of English, had no antibiotics either. So I had a choice: stagger back down the thousands of steps, and then get on a bus to the hospital or stay and weather the illness. I chose the latter. It was the easier yet more dangerous option.

Each day I would go down two hundred odd steps to the cafe and eat one meal, always a dinner of cheese sandwiches or noodles. Cold sweating, I would ask the new faces, whom I hadn't already asked, for antibiotics. They would never have any, so I resorted to staring aimlessly at the faces, feeling lonely. This is the most popular mountain in South East Asia and attracts all nationalities, especially from the rich countries of the world, Americans, Europeans, Aussies, Japanese.

There was the Kiwi who had a school group with him. He had a pretty comprehensive medical kit, which he rummaged deep in, but no antibiotics. All he could give me were throat lozenges. Then there were the Japanese in their droves, with bandannas, ski poles and expensive cameras. They didn't have any either. I started to get angry with all of them but I knew I was angrier with myself for making such an elementary omission.

I was getting to know the staff quite well after six days. Or rather they were getting to know my face and habits and would pre-empt my orders for food. They were young and smartly dressed in cheap clothes, and Bornean in physical features, quite small and, way back, of Chinese origin. I would have to climb back up all those wooden steps after I had eaten my meal, wheezing and feverish. And then I would prop myself up on the veranda and watch the milky coin of the sun sink in the South China Sea behind the islands of Mamutik and Sapi and all the stars race each other for pole position in the darkening sky. The clouds were like the spokes of a bicycle wheel converging on the half sunken golden droplet. One could bathe in the air of the evening, it was so clean but the temperature soon dropped to freezing the moment the sun's bulb died out.

Celia returned in the evening, after dark, and, as I was feeling a little more human, we made plans for our ascent the following day. We weren't bothered about seeing the sun rising and so set off walking at 8 a.m. The tourists looked at us as if we were irresponsible, setting off so late in the day. They were on their way down from the summit just as we were leaving Gunting Lagadan. I climbed up out of the tree line and onto bare rock.

I closed my eyes, the touch of the rock's surface felt like reading Braille, it was so bumpy and rough. I hadn't felt rock for God knows how long. I soaked it up, read it, digested it. I'd felt the plastic of the artificial climbing walls plenty of times recently, but that's no substitute for real rock. It had a friction like no other rock I'd ever touched.

We climbed slowly, up fixed ropes, onto the plateau, Celia holding back for me, like a fit dog straining at the leash. We stopped at Sayat Sayat to load up with what was left, though Celia had already taken just about everything. The clouds were way below us as if we were in a jet plane, soaring, as we passed over the lens of a plateau. That would be a familiar pattern. I trudged wearily past the Donkey's Ears and Low's Peak, without even bothering going to the summit, even though it is the highest point in South East Asia. It seemed strangely irrelevant.

The West Gurkha Hut is down the other side of the lens, below an overhanging phallic piece of rock known as Tetsujin Peak, ideally situated in a perfect cwm with the Dewali Pinnacles on the one side and Nameless Peak on the other. Celia and I planned to climb as many of the twenty-odd peaks as possible during our stay in the West Gurkha. Time was running out for me, having wasted five days being ill, but Celia had climbed quite a few already, though only the ones she could scramble up.

The hut was a pre-fabricated triangle of aluminium with two beds and floor space for two more. We took the floor to be nearer to each other and because of the severely restricted headroom that sleeping on the beds entailed. By pulling the mattresses down from the beds we were able to build a nest for ourselves. There was storage under the beds, the cupboards were well stocked with candles, fuel, spaghetti, rice, and in a locked cupboard Robert New's climbing gear. Contrary to what the ranger told us, there was a generous water supply from two butts filled by run-off from the roof.

I felt stronger right away. Perhaps it was the new surroundings or the illness had run its course, I don't know. The very next morning we got up in darkness, stepping through the ice skinning the puddles like Japanese crackers, and made an attempt on the North West Buttress of Victoria Peak – a 1000 feet of perfect granite the like of which I had never before experienced. Sheer Velcro. You had to peel the shoes off the rock to reposition them. Not even in North America have I touched such rock. I recalled the natural grit edges of the Peak District in Derbyshire, in particular Higgar Tor, rougher than all the other edges, stickier for the shoes.

Celia led off and cranked up to a place about 130 feet directly above me. She wasn't at the right belay and couldn't find it. I began to get irritable immediately and quietly castigated myself for doing so. Climbing second I came up enjoying the movement, though not enjoying taking the camming devices out. They scuffed my knuckles, which I knew would take weeks to heal. I then swung through and got to a ledge twenty feet further on. We got thoroughly professional when we were climbing together and I knew she felt bad about missing the belay ledge but I kept my mouth zipped shut.

I struggled up a thin crack, still feeling the effects of my illness, and belly-flopped onto a ledge. Celia made much easier work of the next pitch, climbing up blocky ground and then thrutching up a chimney where she landed at a spacious sofa. You could see the whole of the South China Sea from that ledge; at least that's how it seemed to us.

'Look. You can see those coral islands where we were. What are they called? Sapi and Mamutik?'

It was my turn again and I was faced with a blank slab fifty feet high. The lower-angled ground beyond gave the whole thing a convex appearance. I stepped onto the rock, feeling the friction with my fingers, which were outstretched, like a pianist's about to perform a concerto. My right foot pedalling the face.

Sharply inhaling I began, sticking to the wall more through faith than any ability I might have. Ever so gently and grotesquely pronated, I pushed the slab away from me to get more weight onto my feet.

Celia mentioned, 'You look very odd.'

I just said, 'Thanks!'

It is important that you trust to friction. Once the seeds of doubt creep into your mind, you can trip on a stumbling block, which could send you off, falling through space. I stayed on, shaking like Mick Jagger, and found easier, blocky ground which led straight to the top. That moment between knowing that you've cracked it and topping out is the moment that climbers search for. That moment when the pulse begins to race and the joy overwhelms you and you slow down wishing that the feeling will never end. That is *the* moment.

Celia joined me and we hugged, all alone on this remote plateau, on the summit of a pointed mountain, at the closing of the day.

I quickly attempted to climb to the South Summit of Victoria Peak without a rope, solo. I rushed at it and wasn't in tune with the rock and when I looked down to find a foothold I suddenly became aware of a 3000-foot chasm below my feet, straight into Low's Gully. I panicked and was forcefully reminded of the occasion when I was soloing on Dinas Mot, in Snowdonia. At that time the rock and I were dancing to different songs also. I set off and, at first, the climbing was easy but then, as it steepened, the grade got progressively more difficult. My palms began sweating and my slippers were having difficulty finding purchase on tiny edges. I very nearly shook myself off the rock. Elbows out, I was sowing the seeds of doubt. With sewing machine legs, I began hyperventilating in an effort to steady myself. I was hundreds of feet above the Pass of Llanberis and though there were climbers, dotted here and there, on different routes, I was thoroughly alone. It would take them hours to get to me and effect a rescue. It would take a fraction of a second to peel off. I was a mere pimple on the back of a giant.

I once saw a tiny male toad spread-eagled on the back of a gigantic female, about as big as a frying pan, in Iguaçu, Brazil. This is how I felt now, high on a summit, above the rainforests of Borneo, arms and legs spread wide on the back of a great big female toad. I could even feel her back's texture, hard and coarse

23

and even spiky to the touch. If I made one wrong move that displeased her, she could toss me off her back with more ease than a bull-rider off a bull. On Dinas Mot I regained my composure and climbed on that day on the Super Direct but here, with the void below me, I reversed off the toad. The time wasn't right and I knew it.

It's a little like reading poetry, soloing is. If I am relaxed, I have no trouble and the words flow but if I am tensed up, it all goes to pot and I begin to stumble over lines. Like trip wires for the tongue. One has to be supremely pacific to move with the grain of the rock and not against it.

The following morning we set off early to explore the slender buttress sweeping down from the summit of Nameless Peak. We failed to climb it after just 130 feet of its 650-foot height. It needed a bolt or bravery to bypass a particularly treacherous wall, and we had neither. That will be one of my biggest regrets, not climbing that pillar. It was the most beautiful piece of rock you could imagine and now, thinking that I'll never climb it, hurts like hell. Perhaps I'll get a team of friends interested in it and have them climb it for me. Maybe, one day, I'll be able to make it up there again and watch, taking photos.

We climbed other peaks around the hut but the most enduring memory for me is scrambling up Victoria Peak in the dark: We set off from the hut under an Indian ink black sky pierced with millions of tiny lights, our head torches by far the biggest. The sound of boots and heavy breathing dominated.

I was doing a sacred *Om* with each exhalation, as an Indian friend taught me, as it would give me more power. Dawn was upon us as we neared the summit and seeing the headlamps of the crowds over on Low's Peak made us giggle and, dare I say it, gloat.

There wasn't a cloud in the sky as we stood on that knife-edged ridge with the whole world below us, arms out, flying in the wind. Even the sun bathed us in its red light from below, as if it were worshipping us, rather than us it. And as it rose higher it cast an immense triangular shadow in the rainforest, 14,000 feet below to the west of the mountain.

This was the start to our round the world tour that I had dreamt of for years. Maybe not the being ill bit, but I had soon forgotten about that. Next stop Australia and then Utah, and so to Alaska. This was the life, a grand in your pocket, six months on the road and not a care in the world.

3

TOWARDS THE TOTE

The man who comes back through the door in the wall will never be quite the same as the man who went out.

Aldous Huxley,
Doors of Perception

Celia always got scared flying and coming in to land at Sydney was no exception. She had her head on my chest and her eyes shut tight. I dreamt back to that time when we were taking off in Punta Arenas in Chilean Patagonia: The wind raged across the runway and we saw the aeroplanes shuddering in the face of it. Wires clattered against sheet metal. As we sat up in the viewing area drinking coffee we watched one of the planes coming in to land. The thing was tilting violently to the left and to the right as it caught the wind. I watched her face as she stared in horror out of that window. Her frailness touched me then, as it did now. She could be so hard sometimes, so impenetrable and these glimpses of her fallibility communicated so much more to me than all her armour.

After we touched down, we got a courtesy bus to a cheap hotel, rented a room with a balcony, showered the journey from us and went straight out to buy a car on the underground car market. The Basement was a peculiar sort of cave, the home of troglodytes for the duration it takes to sell their cars. They were all travellers who breathed diesel fumes for air and squinted as they came up into the light.

We bought a big white Ford Falcon off a German couple who had done the grand tour of the continent in it and were only sentenced to a week down there in the dark before encountering us. There were others who had done six weeks in that dungeon, attempting to sell a car that had taken more of a hammering than Frank Bruno. They were all lined up in ranks, the Austrians with the Datsun, the Irish good time girls with the Nissan and the Swiss with the VW camper. There were about forty of them partying around bottles of beer and joints that made the atmosphere even denser than it was already.

Tourist attractions were ignored one after the other. Even I made a move to see the Opera House, I who had been in Delhi on countless occasions and had yet to make the detour to visit the Taj Mahal. But that was voted against. That's what I loved about Celia, she refused to conform to any rule, had no interest in what the tourists wanted to do.

We cruised off in our big white shed on wheels to our first destination, the Blue Mountains. Only 120 kilometres north of Sydney, the Blueys have a much more remote feel, though they are virtually a suburb of the big city. We spent a week cragging at such places as Cosmic County and Mount Piddington. They reminded me of the Lancashire quarries where I began climbing. All dusty edges and orange and green lichenous rock, square, angular, arêtes and corners, nuts and pegs. One climb in particular put me in the time machine and suddenly there were all my old mates from a decade ago – Nelson, Grids, Shaps, Tim and Big Pete, calling and laughing in the dense and tangled forest, shouting, barracking and taking the piss from the bushes on the deck. Briefly, I missed their broad Lancastrian accents and coarse manners.

Then this American guy, called Bill appeared and invited himself to climb with us. 'There's nobody else here so it looks like I'm climbing with you,' he barked. He had greasy black hair pasted to his balding head and sandals. He was incredibly lanky and climbed with a little black book, which he wrote in every time he did a route. There are these climbers who are obsessive and, just like train-spotters or twitchers, they must record everything.

Pretty soon he was hogging the leads and telling Celia how she should climb. It came to a head when the lead was hers and he started scoffing at her as if it were obvious how she should execute a move.

'You just need to climb straight up there,' he remarked.

Celia damn near bit his head off when she replied, 'I would do if I could reach!' He went strangely quiet.

He was a schoolteacher from the tough side of San Francisco and we reasoned that he was used to ordering the kids around because that's the only way he'd get them to do anything. It's just that it didn't work so well with adults. He had been on several road trips to Australia and we met a fair few people who knew him and made every attempt to steer clear of him. But he had cunning ways of trapping the unsuspecting climber. He changed his vehicle for every trip he did and he had a knack of just looming up out of the foliage. In fact he was the king of the unsuspected loom.

We shook him off eventually. Well, we ran away really, cutting our time short in the Blueys, and cruising off into the sunset. We drove all night and pulled in for breakfast at a Red Rooster, a neon cockerel pointing the way. The food came in cardboard boxes and it was difficult to ascertain where the box ended and the food began.

After an abortive attempt to climb at the Point Perpendicular sea cliffs, where only one route was ascended, we were unceremoniously kicked off. We wondered why we were the only tent on a most beautiful campsite, with its own private beach and private wallabies and kookaburras. Pretty soon a helicopter was hovering over us and a loudhailer was screaming at us, saying that we had ten minutes to clear the area. The Australian equivalent of the RAF were practising their bombing technique and wanted us to shove off. We hurriedly folded up our tent and chairs and cooking stuff and complied. They were practising for a whole week and so even though it was the best weathered, most perfect sandstone we had come across anywhere we thought it wise to leave it to the jet planes. We were not having the luck we were used to.

Lolloping off to Mount Buffalo in South Australia was like crossing the Patagonian Pampa; all rolling hills scorched brown under a searing sun. Cattle and sheep wandered amongst the burnt tree stumps. We arrived in the dead of night and, climbing up the hairpins, surprised a wombat in our lights. We rolled into the campsite to discover it virtually full. Putting up the tent whilst trying not to make a sound was impossible and with our giggling I'm sure we roused lots of campers.

We woke up early because of the cold and were surprised to see snow for we had just come from the baking plains. We watched in awe as tortoise domes and elephantine boulders came to life as shadows shifted with the low sun. We cast our shade onto the surrounding plain. This mountain, being a national park, is heavily forested and there is something quite energising about wandering around in a damp cool forest of eucalyptus, mosses clinging to granite and trunk. But the cool temperatures didn't last very long and it was soon baking at 7000 feet.

Mount Buffalo is a granite mountain not unlike Kinabalu, the difference being the vegetation and the rock texture. No giant pitcher plants or rafflesia here, but there's plenty of eucalyptus. Kinabalu had the most perfect granite either of us had ever climbed on, whereas Mount Buffalo was not dissimilar to a cheese grater, so sharp and big were the crystals. We found this out to our horror on the age-old classic Where Angels Fear to Tread. The route is graded a very moderate 16 and is about nine pitches long.

It begins with a battle up a wide crack on the first pitch which Celia, some might say sensibly, backed off. This didn't put her in a particularly good mood for the rest of the ascent and adding to this was the intense still heat, like an oven. This made our feet swell in our purposefully small shoes and they hurt beyond belief. Our throats parched as we dehydrated and the sweat poured off us in little rivulets. As the tape wore off our hands the cuts started to show and the pain when we attempted a jamming move made us nauseous. I remember the cool updraft on the gorge rim as we emerged, battered, but not beaten, yet.

There was a hang glider taking off from a special ramp on the gorge rim and a sign that read 'NO HANG GLIDING WITHOUT A VALID LICENCE' nailed to a tree. It must have been 3000 vertical feet to the road below us. I remember thinking, God, that looks exhilarating, as she ran into space, fell for a little way, stalled and continued, like a leaf falling from a tree.

During our seven days there we climbed lots of other routes, until our hands were in tatters and we decided to be on our way and visit Melbourne. We had an old friend there.

Glenn Robbins met us on a garage forecourt at night. It was like a shady drugs deal. Both Celia and I were nervous as hell about meeting him. We had parted on bad terms, or not so much bad terms but just with things left unsaid. It was Glenn who had scraped me up and pulled me out of the water at the Gogarth sea cliffs on Anglesey in 1993.

I had fallen whilst climbing in Wen Zawn, a huge amphitheatre of rock the colour of snow, site of such classics as A Dream of White Horses, on a giant slab to one side, and Conan the Librarian on the arch opposite. I was trying to ascend the direct start to The Games Climbers Play, which goes up the impending, jagged wall between these two routes. It was graded modestly at E4, but no one had made a second ascent to confirm this. Normally a climber makes a second ascent to confirm grade and quality, stuff like that, but this climb hadn't been repeated for ten years since it was first done. The route 'belongs' to Pat Littlejohn who is a very good climber and also notorious for his undergrading. So, even though it was graded easy, by my standards, it should have been treated with respect. Over-confidence and a lack of respect was to be my undoing.

Dew or rain was on the grass on top of the crag. No choughs about. Drizzle filled the air. Amidst this miasma Glenn and I abseiled down the damp rock face. The situation felt wrong somehow. But I went along with it, disregarding the now all too obvious signs. Lacing my boots all I could hear was the infernal noise of the waves, crashing into the Zawn. Other times, for I was a regular visitor here, I'd got a kick out of that noise. Uncoiling the ropes, I felt my heart beating in my head like you get when you're coming up on some drug or other. I climbed up ninety feet thinking, this is wrong. I shouldn't be here. And then, sketching on wet rock and pumped to hell, I jumped to avoid falling awkwardly. I wasn't scared because I'd got loads of protection in, the last piece being by my feet. What happened next was a fluke of engineering. As the ropes came tight the nuts, that were on too short quickdraws or slings, lifted out of their placements. Six camming devices ripped from their cracks in the loose rock and the one bomber nut snapped. Afterwards the nut was retrieved by Fred Hall of the equipment manufacturers DMM and the wire examined under a microscope. This revealed that the quickdraw was too short on this nut as well, and when it lifted, as the piece ripped above it, it was sliced through on the sharp edge of the crack.

The result of all this was I hit fins of rock feet-first and then somersaulted into a narrow cleft head-first. This cleft wasn't wide enough for my shoulders to fit into but it was full of water. Glenn had to free himself from the system and climb down to me, which would have taken five to ten minutes. He then had to pull me out feet-first and resuscitate me. I was having some sort of near death experience, because I had practically drowned, but none of it included any lights at the end of any tunnels. Maybe I hadn't gone far enough down it, though it felt as if I had. I was lying in summer grass; I could tell it was summer because the evening was warm and the grass very long. Hedgerows were all around me and I could hear the buzzing of bees and children playing. Then it began to grow dark, very dark and it felt like there wasn't anything there, like the opposite of a religious experience.

In reality there was effectively no way out. We had abseiled in and were planning to climb out again. And anyway how could he leave me alone, for all he knew I could have been dying. It must have been a desperately worrying time for Glenn, who luckily for me is a trained lifeguard. He had wrapped me in his own jacket and waistcoat to stall the hypothermia but could do no more. We were the only people in Wen Zawn and the chances of being rescued before dark were virtually non-existent. As night time came, we would be noticed by our absence and friends would ask, 'Where the hell are Glenn and Paul?' For five hours we were down there, where that rock met the sea, before Olly Saunders, out walking his dog in a spot where not many dog-walkers venture, spotted the frantically waving Glenn. Another hour and air, land and sea rescue services were called into action. On top of the crag were the butcher, the baker, the ferry-money taker from Holyhead, all out just in case. There was a lifeboat in the swell and a helicopter in the grey mist also.

I was strapped into a stretcher, handled into a dinghy by men who were strangely expressionless and, through the swell, taken to a waiting lifeboat. I was then winched onto the deck and almost immediately winched up into a hovering helicopter. An oxygen mask was snapped onto my face and the chronic pain stabbing at my chest disappeared. Within twenty minutes I was in hospital being wheeled through long corridors on a stretcher. In my hypothermic state the blanket felt toasty. I remember puking on Zoe, like a baby fulmar when it feels threatened. She was my landlady but also an old friend who came straight down the moment she heard about my fall.

The list of injuries were numerous and significant. I had broken my ankle, dislocated both my shoulders, fractured my skull and aspirated Holyhead's finest seawater. The Irish Sea on which Holyhead is a port is renowned for being the dirtiest sea in Britain and I had drowned in it. For two weeks I was in hospital with a badly infected chest.

One day the hospital secretary handed me the telephone and there was Glenn on the other end. He hadn't been in to see me the last two weeks and I wondered why. Apparently he had taken to drinking heavily since the accident; he was in deep shock and needed some kind of trauma counselling. That's what I'd heard from my other friends.

'Royt, you cant. What's all this about moy clawthes, thin?' he ranted. 'Me black jackut and black woistcawt, what's happened to thim?'

The doctors had cut them off me, as is normal, so they don't have to drag your limbs everywhere. They were in a black plastic bin bag, all cut up. Confused, I couldn't answer him. Only now, in Melbourne, did I find out that the clothes didn't matter to him. He was lashing out at me because I was getting all the attention and he was virtually being ignored. That's how it seemed to him, anyway. I had hung up the receiver and started to blubber like a child. So muddled was my brain that I didn't know what was going on. I learned that he was behaving peculiarly towards everyone who thought of him as a friend, slagging mates off behind their backs and ignoring others in the pub.

I discharged myself, against the will of the nursing staff, thinking that I would be fine at Zoe's house. I was still suffering heavily from concussion and the drunken binges that followed weren't to help matters. Eventually my mum came to the rescue and, finding me languishing on some beanbags, took me in. It was dreamy to sleep in my childhood bedroom and I think it made my mum feel useful again after all these years, being able to cook for me and spoil me.

Glenn flew home to Victoria in late '93 and we hadn't heard anything about him since. He was similarly nervous about meeting us, I could sense it. He had totally and purposefully distanced himself from the climbing scene ever since and because of that accident. He spends his time now making ceramics and tending to his bonsai trees with the same vigour and discipline he used to put into his climbing photography.

Glenn soon relaxed and so did we. It was just like old times again. He showed us the sights of Melbourne, namely the tallest building in the city and the biggest mall in the world. And we vegged out to what he termed splat movies like *Natural Born Killers* and *Hellraiser* on the video. But after a couple of days one gets fed up with city life and yearns for a fix of wilderness again. Mount Arapiles, near Natimuk, was to be our next destination but the temperature was an incredible forty-five degrees celcius there. So that is when we decided to go to Tasmania and wait for Arapiles to cool down some.

We took an overnight boat across the Bass Strait and watched from the deck as we came in to port. It looked almost exactly the same as coming in to dock at an Outer Hebridean port like Storna-way on Lewis. This made us feel at home for we've travelled and sailed throughout these islands.

The arrival in Tasmania was followed by a six-hour drive straight to Fortescue Bay on the southern tip of the Tasman Peninsula. Parking up at the bay campsite at 3 p.m., we located the trail, and sprinted straight off. We knew Alun Hughes, Caradog and Deri Jones were making a film about the Totem Pole right about now for S4C, the national television station for Wales. We had made a date to meet them on the Pole. We ran virtually all the eight kilometres. I took the rucksack and sent Celia running ahead. She was still fitter than I, with all the load carrying she had done on Kinabalu while I was ill in that cell. I had been slow to regain lost strength but apparently it isn't good to get it back too quickly.

You can't even see the Totem Pole until you are literally upon it. You peer over the cliff edge lying on your belly, scared to stand upright in case you should teeter and fall. And there's this narrow cleft with seawater flushing through it, well over 300 feet below. About 130 feet away, across the cleft, stands the Candlestick, another sea stack which is even higher than where we were stand-ing. Between the two is a pinnacle that I found hard to believe was the fabled Totem Pole, so insignificant is it compared to the cliffs around it.

Looking down a full 200 feet I could make out the figure of Caradog, or Crag to those that know him, standing on a ledge just below the top of the thing. I was so excited that I shouted, without thinking of Alun, who could have been filming. But when I apologised he said not to worry, the waves were louder than I was.

Once I'd scrambled down the track to where Celia was waiting I could get a better impression of the stack. Only twelve feet wide and 200 feet high, it certainly is the most slender sea stack in the world. It's hard to believe it has remained standing for so long. Its days must be numbered. I could see in my mind's eye the waves that must come crashing through that narrowing in the rock. If you took a needle and enlarged it proportionately to 200 feet this is what you've got. I mentally threaded the Free Route up it. From the sketch I had studied so often I could make out the start from the dry rock, the traverse, the belay ledge and the arête. There is a certain joy to doing this, you get a feel for the route and it gives you something in return to visualise. You build up a relationship. You and the rock.

This route would be all consuming now, would captivate me, until I did it. But there's something else. You can see where the routes don't go. This makes it possible to spy out imaginary new lines, ways you would like to climb. I can't resist sussing out new routes. For me it's one of the joys of rock climbing.

It was handshakes and hugs all round. We hadn't really expected to meet these guys from back home all this distance away. The chances of meeting up on a remote sea stack miles from anywhere are pretty slim and to get the timing right is leaving even more to chance. We were introduced to their two Tasmanian helpers, and we climbed into an aluminium motor boat, driven by a real Boy Racer who would try to get air off each wave, which meant that we would come crashing down into the troughs. After the eight-kilometre ride we all had sore arses and necks. He approached the jetty going at high speed and, telling us to hold on tight, performed an emergency stop, rather like a hand brake turn, just short of the wooden structure.

There then followed miles of driving, in convoy down typical

Australian dirt roads. For the amount of people using these roads it isn't worth surfacing them, so the whole continent is threaded with tracks of red earth. An invitation to stay with the guys was readily forthcoming, and we jumped at the offer, the alternative being the rather expensive campground at Fortescue Bay. Once on the surfaced road we drove past Port Arthur. This tourist attraction was an old penal colony, where Martin Bryant had a brainstorm and killed thirty-five people back in '96. Everybody seems to know someone who has a relative who was murdered by that guy, there are so few people living in the place.

Once inside the chalet we realised just how small it was and decided to pitch our tent on the balcony to give the others some space. There was a guy who we hadn't seen before who had shoulder-length blond hair, a cut-off shirt so typical of many Aussie males, an immensely muscular torso and upper legs leading to matchstick thin lower legs supported by callipers. He was wearing shorts and I couldn't keep my eyes off his legs. He was definitely the leader of the team, the elder, and talked about walking in to Mount Brown and Frenchman's Cap. Frenchman's is a twelve-hour hike from the roadhead through bog and tussocks and he seemed to have climbed every route there. So obviously his disability didn't stop him in any way.

He was very cagey at first and I remember thinking, has this guy got a chip on his shoulder or what? I only asked him if he knew of any new routes to go and attempt and I remember being shocked at his reply. 'There's plenty of existing routes to do before you start looking for new ones.'

It was as if he was trying to put me off the scent, trying to steer me away from the new routes. This only served to fire me up more. 'So there *are* new routes up there?'

'Are you one of these guys who wants to make a name for yourself?' I thought about that for a second. I didn't need more than a second because I knew that I was. 'Because Tassie's not the place for it.'

I think that head on response is the Tasmanian way. Every

Tasmanian we had met during our stay there had a certain brashness about them. They were very kind though and absolutely refused to let us buy any food in. The Boy Racer cooked us abalone, which was exquisite. Living in such close proximity to the sea every family has a fishing boat and every child goes on fishing trips.

I later found out the blond guy who was giving me a hard time was called Pete Steane. When he left I asked the Boy Racer about him. 'What happened to his legs? A climbing accident?'

'Yeah, he took a fall while climbing on the Pipes. He landed on his back and the trigger bar of a Friend punctured his spinal cord.'

The Organ Pipes, I discovered, is a climbing area on the flank of Mount Wellington, above Hobart.

'How long ago was the accident, then?' I probed.

' 'Bout ten, maybe more, years. He was paralysed in the whole of his legs at first but then slowly, over years, he's regained movement.'

Morning broke and we got up seriously early for the filming to take place. We were to hitch a ride with them to the Moui, a much stumpier sea stack than the Totem Pole, across the other side of Fortescue Bay. The Moui, which is the name given to the Easter Island statues, though of less stature than the Totem Pole, is still an incredible stack. Perched on a plinth, it doesn't take the tide like the Tote but is much more remote, especially if you have to bushwhack.

We were landed at the base of the Moui and got ashore by grabbing hold of seaweed roots and scrambling up greasy rock. The boys then left us to ourselves. Celia uncoiled the ropes on a clean bit of basalt, sat on her trainers and, lacing her climbing shoes up tight, chose the protection she needed for the route by looking up at it and then down at her rack. We had travelled light on this climb and chose just the bare essentials, one set of cams, one set of nuts and ten quickdraws. She climbed first, moving gracefully up the tower and I followed, revelling in the act. Before abseiling off she showed me a school of dolphins cutting through the sea in perfect arcs.

I chose a harder line because it involved laybacking with the right hand, exactly the same moves as the Totem Pole. I figured that if I practised this enough the Tote would be no problem. Anyway I fell off it but felt that I was close to doing the moves. A second try proved me right. We didn't have to wait long for the pickup and we were back on the Boy Racer rodeo again. I swear, up until a week later, I'd never had such pain in my neck, back or arse.

We then took off in our Ford Falcon across the Tasman Peninsula to Hobart, and then up to Mount Wellington. Mount Wellington overlooks Hobart with its expansive natural harbour; you can drive to the very top. It is a popular viewing spot for the tourists and appears to have a large rocket on its summit that is a mast. Tasmania has extremes of climate like no other place I've visited (and Patagonia is said to be 'el Pais de Quatro Estaciones' or 'the Country of Four Seasons'). It can be sunny and baking one moment and suddenly a wind will blow up from the south, the clouds will roll in and the climate will turn truly icy.

We set up home in a hut, about halfway up the mountain, which is used by picnickers when just such an icy wind blows in. Some kind soul had even left us firewood and we got a blaze going in the fireplace. Unfortunately, a team of possums, perhaps led in by the warmth, had the same idea and cuddled up to us in our sleeping bags. We got worried that they might be host to fleas and spent the entire evening scratching with paranoia. What more could we want, a roof over our head, fire in the grate, food in our bellies and, if we shuffled to the edge of the car park, a superb view of the city at night.

We climbed all the next day and the day after that on not such perfect rock as we had come to expect from our tour of Australia. But the situation and positions we found ourselves in more than made up for any failing in quality. From a belay on Neon God, one of the routes we climbed, we saw the QE2 coming in to dock. The funnel was taller than any building in Hobart, which is saying something about Hobart rather than the *QE2*. Then came the tall ships on their round the world voyage. We had to descend to the city to see those up close. Salamanca, the local street market, was overflowing with people, all there to enjoy the spectacle, and the harbour was crowded with dinghies buzzing around to get a better view. The Malaysian Navy were dressed in pirates' garb and swarming all over the rigging. Folk on the quayside threw sweets to the crew as they played frantic pipe music. We ate ice creams and wandered in and out of the crowd who were cheering the ships off as they left.

Next day we were back on Mount Wellington and, like a man obsessed, I was busy choosing arêtes to ascend. I found a couple that involved right-handed laybacking but I think I exhausted the possibilities of climbs requiring this technique. The moment could not be put off any longer. I knew that the tides were just about perfect and I felt ready for the Tote.

4

THE TOTEM POLE

Whatever way one cares to look at it the Tower brings bad news. There is definitely going to be some sort of loss, even a calamity of some kind. Security, as the questioner has known it in the past, is going to be destroyed and the troubles are going to come amazingly quickly when they start. There will be a questioning of previously accepted beliefs, trust will be destroyed. There could even be some sort of disgrace.

Julia and David Line,
A Guide to Fortune Telling with Tarot Cards

The day dawned cloudy and blustery. Celia and I ate banana, mango and oats, filled the Nalgene bottles from the outside tap of the toilet block, slung our rucsacs on our backs and walked off up the narrow track. The path wound all over the place and up and over fallen trees. We met Bristol climber and now Australian resident Steve Monks and American Enga Lokey soon after we had left the campground. Steve was a member of the only team to have free climbed the Totem Pole in 1995 with Simon Mentz, Jane Wilkinson and Simon Carter, and we were going to attempt a second ascent. I knew Steve quite well, though Celia better than I. This pair were incredibly muscular and I was struck by how alike they looked with their aquiline profiles and cheery smiles as they wished us luck, Steve still with his Bristol harmony and Enga in her New Orleans twang.

As soon as we climbed up a steep hill we were rewarded with fantastic views of the ocean. It was well worth the gasping effort of getting up there. Through a gap in the forest we could see the whole, eight-kilometre length of Cape Hauy beneath us. And beyond, there was only the Southern Ocean separating us from the great continent of Antarctica. I imagined icebergs drifting up, but knew they didn't reach as far as here. We were on the look out for killer whales and sharks, as I had heard of sperm whale sightings hereabouts.

I ran down the wooded hillside in my sandals, almost twisting both my ankles again and again as I picked up speed in my urgency to get to the Pole. I was so excited. Ever since I'd seen Simon Carter's photograph published as a poster in *High* magazine I knew I was going to be there. One day. It just had inevitability about it, as it had been inevitable that I was going to give Mount Asgard on Baffin Island my best shot, or that it was Trango Tower, in Pakistan, that held my attention for twelve years.

It was John Ewbank and Allan Keller who made the first ascent of the Totem Pole back in 1968. Their route is a masterpiece of its time. 'I wish some day to make a route and from the summit let fall a drop of water and this is where my route will have gone,' said the Italian 'artist of the mountains' Emilio Comici, and this is what Ewbank and Keller have done.

There were just the two of us on the trail that day. I turned around and Celia was out of sight, behind me. I opened my water bottle and took a deep draught, all the time conscious of preserving the litre of water that I was carrying. There would be no more water from here on in and we would have to ration it. She wasn't very far behind and when she pulled up she sat down too and took a swig from my canteen. Our tee-shirts were soaked in sweat.

The trail wound back on itself and, at times, it would go under a tree trunk too high to climb over and too low to walk under comfortably. This problem I solved by taking the rucsac off my back and pulling it behind me whilst squeezing underneath. At times the path went right along the dizzy edge of the huge cliffs which ring this peninsula. If the ancient aborigines had built promontory forts this would have been the perfect place as it is guarded on three sides by 400-foot walls of columnar diorite.

Thinking I was being smart I took a short cut but the narrow track petered out after only a 150 yards of steep downhill. A choice presented itself, retrace my steps climbing onto tree roots and loose leaves or forge onwards through dense undergrowth. I never liked retracing my steps, especially if it's up a hill. So, ever the eager explorer, I chose the latter. Much to my chagrin, it appeared easier only because it was downhill. Celia was much more sensible and stuck to the path we knew. Needless to say she was waiting at the racking up spot for a good half-hour while I was battling through dense undergrowth. I was all cut up and sweating buckets when I finally emerged to greet her.

We racked up in silence. It's always a tense time, racking up. You tell yourself that you're sure you've forgotten something. You double-check the hardware of which there was painfully little on this route, only the minimum of carrots. Carrots are an Australian speciality that you don't find any place else. That is because there is no cheapskate like an Australian climber. We felt like we were getting the hang of these after a month in Oz. A quarter inch hole is drilled and filled with a steel bolt but no hanger or eye is fitted to it. So you don't have anything to clip the rope to for your safety. You must carry keyhole hangers in your chalk bag, which you slip over the top of the carrot before it is clipped. Many a climber has taken a whipper due to running out of strength whilst fiddling in vain to get a carrot clipped. Or fumbling and dropping the last hanger whilst throwing a whitey.

There are the ropes to be checked for nicks. You put your legs through the harness leg loops and synch up the belt. You check that you've enough chalk in your bag and count the hangers. Make sure your bootlaces are done up nice and tight and, if you are wearing one, make sure your helmet is fitting OK. A last check of your rack and you're off to begin climbing.

Celia was nervous. I attempted to make conversation – 'We seem pretty lucky with the weather' – but she wasn't having any of it. It was then that I realised that she didn't want to be there at all. She was doing this for me and me alone. I had been so selfish that I hadn't seen it in her or, to put it more succinctly, chose not to see it in her before, such was my obsession. Whenever I was involved in a climbing project I was completely obsessed, from the beginning until its completion. I scrambled down to the viewing boulder where I could see if the tide was submerging the only dry rock or not. The rock was dry.

There was still a Tyrolean rope traverse set up across the narrow gap to the summit of the Totem Pole. It's not normally there, just for filming purposes. In my selfishness I traversed first to reach the top of the climb that was to be my chief prize on this trip. Suddenly I was 200 feet above a thrashing swell, not knowing to what the other side of the rope was attached or if the previous climber knew anything about tying knots. I trusted the Welsh guys though. Almost instantaneously I found myself halfway along because the first half is downhill. Fortunately, Celia had the presence of mind to belay me on an extra rope and it was just as well as the existing rope chaffed alarmingly on the edge of the ledge, which protruded below the knot.

The tormented water had the consistency of a creamy head of beer and lumps were breaking off and flying round and round in the wind that was rushing through the narrow channel. I felt nervous for the first time. It was a mad perspective from where I was hanging. The tower's twelve-foot width seemed to taper to nothing at the base and it felt strange that it should still be standing. If you know anything about rope techniques you will be aware that a Tyrolean traverse puts huge amounts of stress on the anchors, much more than a straight hang. I started to have visions of my pulling the Totem Pole over and the whole ensuing catastrophe.

Clamping the jumars on the rope I rushed up the remaining distance as if there were some demonic force at my heels. Celia pulled the jumars back across the rope and then followed, sliding down to the lowest point and taking some photos. We were in a happier mood now that the exhilaration had taken hold of us and we both chattered without hearing what the other was saying. It seemed rather strange to be on the summit first and then to descend from it only to climb up to it again. But the alternative was far more hazardous, or so we believed. This involved rappelling down the cliffs opposite, which appeared to be covered in loose rocks, and hopping from boulder to boulder to reach the base of the stack. At least we were now on the most wave-blasted, wind-sculptured, solid piece of rock on the planet.

The rope danced in the updraft as if it were some uncontrollable serpent as we cast it loose. I put my descender on the rope and slid over the edge, watching Celia's face depart. Down the arête I went, quickly so as not to see anything. It is said to be a far better ascent when there is no prior knowledge of the climb. The more intimately you know each hand hold and foot hold, the less your ascent is rated by the cognoscenti. I arrived at a ledge, about twelve feet by three, which was to be used as our only belay, the climb being two pitches long. Putting a long sling on a carrot as a directional, to hold the rope where I wanted it, I carried on down the last 100 feet. I could look all I wanted now, as the existing climb goes around the other side of the stack. This was new rock, a line which I'd seen from above, a thin crack petering down to nothing. The start looked horrifying and smooth.

There was one arête out of the four that I had to swing around and it took me a couple of tries, down below the high water mark. I was aiming for a two-foot dry patch on a half-drowned boulder alongside the Totem Pole – dry meaning damp but not submerged. As soon as I landed I commenced fighting for my balance on the seaweed-greased rock, first sticking my crotch out and then my arse. All the while my arms behaved like the crazy cop in the silent movies who is trying to stop Harold Lloyd's motor car.

The next minute I was up to my waist in the sea that was flushing through the narrow channel. I couldn't believe my bad luck. We only had one try at this and I had just blown it. I would be hypothermic soon if I didn't get out of these soaking clothes and, besides, my boots and rope were wet and my chalk bag was full of water.

I shouted up to Celia at the top of my voice, 'COME DOWN TO THE LEDGE AND TIE THE ROPE OFF.' I figured that if we were to be denied the first pitch we might as well have a stab at the top one. But she couldn't hear me and I could just make out a distant 'Wha-a-at?' carried away on the wind. The difficulty in hearing each other was due to the crashing waves which sounded like a whole pride of lions roaring. After screaming at each other for a while longer she understood and rappelled down to the halfway point, tying the rope off there. I fixed my jumar clamps onto the line and took in the slack, which is about two moves on the rope. I cut loose in a swing off the greasy seaweed-covered boulder. I had to tuck my knees up to avoid getting my feet in the water as I flew around the arête ... And that is the last thing I remember – until I came around with an unearthly groan.

When I regained consciousness I was upside down, confused and there was blood pissing out of my head. I was immediately aware of the gravity of the situation. I needed to get back upright if I was to stem the flow of blood, so I concentrated on shrugging my pack off. Once off, I tried again and again to get myself sitting up in my harness but failed miserably. I was too weak and strangely uncoordinated. I gazed despondently down from an obtuse angle at the orange stain spreading in the salt water. I had a moment to reflect on what seemed to be my last view: a narrow corridor of pale grey cloud flanked by two black walls, with the white foam of the sea, which was turning quickly red, right there by my head as a ceiling to my fear. I could feel the life's blood draining out of me, literally, and there was nothing I could do about it.

Suddenly Celia was there, by me, telling me sweet lies about how it was all going to be OK.

'I heard a splash,' she said in her Buckinghamshire-cum-Yorkshire accent. 'You've taken a little rock on your head but you've had worse.'

It's funny but those untruths are extremely comforting in moments like these. It's like you want to believe them, so you do. I was still hanging below the high water mark and had an irrational fear about my blood attracting sharks, never mind drowning when the tide turned. Imagine being engulfed by the tide and, ever so slowly, being overcome as the water rises inch by creeping inch. I was now in a fluffy dream world with cotton wool inside my head. Muffled voices were all about me and yet I was sure that only Celia was present. She fought to get me upright in slings and put her helmet on my head when she saw what a mess I'd made of it (several months later, in the back of an ambulance, I happened across the surgeon's report which stated that there was 'much brain oozing out').

She prussiked the 100 feet back up to the ledge and rigged up a simple two-way pulley system through a karabiner. When I say simple, what I really mean is anything but simple, especially with only one bolt to use. It is just the simplest pulley system you can have. Now I weigh ten and a half stone (147 pounds) and she weighs nine stone (126 pounds), so you may ask how is this humanly possible? You must have heard about the child who lifted a car off her father who was being crushed when a jack failed. There are numerous such stories of superhuman strength fuelled by adrenaline. I can only put this in the same category. She says it was hard, but it had to be done, she had no choice in the matter. She either did it or I died. So there was no decision to make.

Celia struggled in desperation for three hours to get me up to the ledge but faltered at the last hurdle. There was a right-angled edge to be surmounted to get me onto the ledge and the harder she pulled the tighter the rope became without moving me.

'You've got to help me here if we're to get you out of this,' she barked. It was the first time I'd heard her lose her composure over this whole episode. I tried to placate her by telling her not to worry but a tired moan was all that came out of my mouth. Then was the first time I noticed something amiss with the limbs on my right side – well, I couldn't so much tell which side it was.

I only knew that they had no feeling in them at all and however much I tried I couldn't move them. My arm was being thrashed around like a rag doll's and my leg was sustaining deep wounds as shinbone scraped sharp rock. I looked down at my leg and couldn't work out why it wasn't able to move. It was like a piece of wood, a cricket bat, for instance, being knocked on the edge of a stone tabletop. I remember thinking that it was just a temporary lapse in control of my body and I would soon be back to normal. With my left arm and leg I fought my way onto the ledge, first my chest, then my belly, then my legs. I lay exhausted on my front and all I could think about was going to sleep.

Celia put me in the recovery position (essentially lying on your front with your head turned to one side, a position that keeps your airway open and is sure to eject vomit). She gave me a hug, then told me she was going to have to leave me and get help. I was terrified that it was the last time I was going to see her but I didn't show my feelings. She was probably thinking the same thoughts. Celia then jumared back up the final 100 feet of the stack and crossed the Tyrolean traverse where I heard her shouting encouraging words. I answered with a groan, which she certainly could not hear.

The first time I met Celia was on a remote Scottish island. We went crazy. It was midsummer and light virtually all night long. It feels, in my vague memory, like we never slept, just partied round the clock. We soon got a reputation as the party crew, locals would turn up on tractors, their trailers loaded with ale at six o'clock in the morning. We joined the football team, playing on a cow field by the beach, with a dark silhouette of the Cuillin of Rhum just across the water. Eigg vs Muck. Taking part in the village ceilaidh, we spun each other drunkenly around until we stopped spinning and only the room was left revolving.

Ed Stone and I had a plan to free climb the 'last great aid route' in these islands, the Sgurr of Eigg. The Sgurr is a huge prow of columnar basalt, looking not so dissimilar to Venezuela's Mount Roraima, the fabled Lost World of Conan Doyle. Our ascent ended spectacularly when I fell off, clutching a colossal block. We decided to admit defeat and enjoy the midsummer madness for the rest of the week.

I fell hopelessly in love with Celia as soon as I set my eyes on her. It was her moodiness that intrigued me and I made notes about her in my little green book. She has high cheekbones, steel blue eyes, full lips and a wonky nose. Back then she had permed blond hair. We gazed at each other across the campfire and went skinny-dipping on our private beach. She would often climb up into a tree and sulk about I didn't know what and didn't like to ask. It would be a further two years before we got it together.

The seven hours that followed on the Tote were a fight to stay awake when all I wanted to do was drift into unconsciousness. But I was convinced that if I went to sleep I would surely die. Blood was pooling on the ledge from under Celia's helmet and I was blinded in my left eye. I foolishly put my hand under the hard hat to feel the damage for myself, and when I removed it, amidst the blood, there appeared to be a clear liquid which only served to confuse my already addled brain. I began talking to myself: 'Hmmm, what have we here then?' I answered myself: 'It looks as if you have a mighty hole in your head there, Mr Pritch-ard.' I remember having the image of a soft-boiled egg and toast soldiers just before blacking out for the first time.

Meanwhile Celia was running the eight kilometres back to the campsite, not knowing whether I was alive or dead. She met a couple of New South Walean climbers on the path who were coming to have a look at the Totem Pole and she pleaded with them to come down to be with me. As they had all their equipment with them they were very willing to oblige. They shouted, to see if I was still alive from the cliff top, but I still couldn't answer. I suspect it was a corpse they were expecting to encounter when they finally rappelled in to me. Later I learnt their names from the Tasmania Police report: Tom Jamieson and Andrew Davidson. I don't remember their faces but I felt their presence and heard their kind concerned voices.

I could now hear the all too familiar sound of helicopter rotor blades on the wind. The wind had been steadily picking up speed since we arrived and was now blowing through the narrow canyon with some force. I don't know the exact sequence of events. They appeared completely irrelevant to me and yet directly concerned me at the same time. I had chosen probably the most difficult place to get rescued on the whole coastline of Southern Tasmania. A twelve by 200-foot sea stack in the middle of a 160-foot channel with 400-foot cliffs on either side. And I was stuck on a ledge exactly halfway up it. A helicopter rescue was out of the question; it was just too dangerous, the rotor blades coming perilously close to the sidewalls.

Neale Smith, the only climbing paramedic in the whole of Tasmania, happened to be on duty that day and this was to be my one and only lucky break. He set about traversing the Tyrolean rope bridge and rappelling down to the New South Walean climbers and me. Meanwhile a rescue boat was radioed and on its way from Nubeena, about twenty-five kilometres away, that was our only hope of a rescue before dark. He sat by me for a couple of hours, with reassuring words, until I heard, as if in a dream, the screeching sound of a motor boat in the channel below. The boat handler had to negotiate submerged rocks at a depth of just a few feet. He then had to steer the craft in to the very base of the stack so that Neale could abseil down with me clipped to him, all the while trying not to disturb my head.

I remember being in the vertical again, not knowing at the time that here was the only guy of the paramedic team who knew how to perform such a technical operation. A blurred black wall was passing me by for what appeared to be an eternity. I remember being handled into the aluminium tub by the crew. What felt like a hundred hands groped me and attempted to make me comfortable. 'Cut his harness off him,' I heard one of the rescue team say as the driver skilfully slalomed in and out of the sunken rocks. Ian Kingston, the pilot, has since been nominated for a medal by the Tasmania Police Force, as has Celia for her bravery and skill.

It wasn't as pleasant a ride as we had taken with the Boy Racer and that is saying something. We battered up and down on each wave with people trying to hold me still in an attempt at stopping me being flung from the boat. The deafening whine of the outboard as it tore through the water still haunts me. There are times, as I write this book, when a lawn mower passes by the Rehab Unit window that for apparently no reason a shiver will run down my spine and I begin shaking. At the beach in Fortescue Bay I knew I was going to see Celia and made an attempt to compose myself and straighten my hair, which consisted of smearing the blood all over my face. Obviously she still didn't know if I had made it and it was with a certain relief that she saw me still hanging in there.

A stretcher was carried out of the boat and in to a helicopter, apparently with me in it, and it flew to the Cambridge Airport, about 100 kilometres distant. We couldn't fly direct to the Hobart Great War Memorial before getting picked up by ambulance, as is normally the case, because it is illegal to fly around the city after dark. I was then rushed by 'ambo' across the Tasman Bridge to the Royal Hobart Hospital. I had seen this place many times because it is right there on the street corner; you pass it every time you leave or enter the city. I just have this image of concentric rows of windows and a fountain outside the main door. The stretcher was then put on a trolley and wheeled into the hospital. I recall the ceilings of corridors and lots of distorted faces as they stared down at me from twelve inches; ever so bright pen torches being shone into my eyes.

The paramedics decided against a morphine injection as it depresses the nervous system. Apparently they never administer opiates with head injuries. I wasn't in pain as such anyway, just out of it from blood-loss; I'm told there are no pain receptors in the brain. The surgeon's report reads that: 'On arrival the patient was still conscious but grossly dysphasic with right sided hemiplegia', or to put it more simply, unable to speak and paralysed down one side. Celia arrived a couple of hours later, alone and by car. Again she expected to be told, 'Sorry we've lost him. We did all we could.' But I was in the operating theatre and still hanging on in there. When the nurses were preparing me for surgery they took Celia's helmet off me and found that my brains were literally hanging out of the ten by five-centimetre hole in my skull. I was still in wet clothes and the doctor rebuked Neale for not undressing me. I don't know what he could have dressed me in alternatively. My long hair had to be shorn and two litres of blood transfused. The surgeon worked for six hours, in the dead of night, picking shards of bone and rock from the inside of my head.

The accident occurred on a Friday, which also happened to be the 13th February. As a rule I'm not a superstitious person and I still am not. I will walk under ladders or do dangerous things on the 13th just to tempt fate. Nothing has changed, only that I feel a slight uneasiness on subsequent Friday the 13ths. This new day was Saint Valentine's day. While lovers were exchanging pink gifts I was on the operating table having an 'intracerebral haemorrhagic contusion' removed from my brain with a little vacuum cleaner in an operation known as an osteoclastic craniotomy. There were scans taken before and after the operation. The post-operative scan showed the 'removal of bony fragments over the vertex after the evacuation (Hoovering) of a left fronto-parietal lobe haematoma (clot)'.

Celia began the grim business of telephoning our friends and family to warn them that I might not make it. It was morning back home. She was careful to get the news to my parents first so they wouldn't hear it second hand. My friends' attempts to rationalise their sorrow manifested itself in a number of ways. Possibly the most bizarre attempt was Adam Wainwright's going climbing that very day on Craig Doris, perhaps the loosest sea cliff in Wales and not wearing a helmet! I climbed Trango Tower in the Karakoram with Adam, which makes him a particularly good friend. One can't go through something like a major climb without some special bond developing. My father, mother, sister and brother all cried when they heard the bad news. Tracey, my sister who lives in Lebanon, offered to fly out to Tasmania with my mother. They all knew there was a chance I could die and they prepared for it in a number of ways.

Later my mother described how it felt like the bottom was falling out of her world, and how she lay on the bed shaking and sobbing at the prospect of losing a son. Afterward this was my deepest regret, more than never being able to climb again or run or even walk. Putting her through such a traumatic event was unforgivable. She telephoned my dad who did weep but he's much too much of a man to admit it. He went about his allotment with a hollow feeling in his stomach and lost weight through worry. Tracey prayed for me, and her husband, Kim, contacted Greg, a parson friend of his in Hobart who would shortly come and visit me. In fact there were people praying for me in Malaysia, where Kim's parents live, in Lebanon, where my sister and her husband work as missionaries, in Bolton, my home town, and in Hobart itself where Greg the parson's Taroona church congregation would pray for me whenever they met.

Obviously I wasn't aware of any of these goings on, as I was unconscious or hallucinating wildly for the best part of four days. When I awoke on the intensive care unit I had no idea where I was or that the course of my life had been drastically altered in one second. That's all it takes for a rock to impact.

5

HDU

A sudden relinquishment, and perhaps exhaustion, of feeling –
for profound and passionate feelings were no longer needed, no
longer suited to my changed and, so to speak, prosaic position
– so different from the tragedy, comedy and poetry of the
mountain. I had returned to the prose, the everydayness, and,
yes, the pettiness of the world.

Oliver Sacks,
A Leg to Stand On

As if by some cruel joke my bed was placed dead opposite the
window, which looked straight over the roof tops, with a full
view of the Organ Pipes. There was a skate boarder on a billboard,
pulling a one-handed handstand on the lip of a half pipe, whilst
advertising Coca-Cola with the other. He was grinning at me
from his upside-down stance. I was in the Neurological High
Dependency Unit of the Royal Hobart Hospital.

After a few days I could make out the routes I had climbed a
week previously, they were so close – the arête and the corner,
the crack and the chimney. I could see the blurred and winding
road curling up there and just make out the shed which we slept
in with the possums. Higher up, on the summit, I could see,
through a haze, the antennae like a space rocket.

It had been five days since the Accident and I was starting to
get a clearer picture of what I'd done to myself. I'd had two other
hideous accidents but neither of these could remotely compare to
what I was going through now. Neither could be said to be a

capital letter Accident. But I believe that without that previous experience of trauma I would probably have died. I would have expired alone on that ledge were it not for the fighting to stay awake while the life's blood drained out of me. I relaxed and didn't panic, conserving my energy, that was the fight. That's what I'd learnt that day at Gogarth with Glenn Robbins and on Creagh Meaghaidh with Nick Kekus, that you have to put yourself into a trance-like state, slow down, although this possibly happens naturally, if you are to survive.

I still couldn't speak or move my right side. My face felt numb, like the right-hand side wasn't moving. I rang for a nurse and embarked on an almighty game of charades, but she didn't understand all my pointings at a plate, at my reflection in the stainless steel cot side and back at my face. All I wanted to ask for was a mirror. I was left exhausted. She thought I wanted food and then something to do with the cot sides. I think she was just as frustrated as I was at not being able to guess what I was on about.

I was desperate to see my face. It felt numb and swollen, my eye was almost closed and I still had blurred vision. I was dribbling saliva out of the right side of my mouth and I could just make out the looks on the faces of my few visitors, which registered pity and compassion or shock and horror. I felt like a real life Quasimodo.

Tubes still came out of my neck and nose and cock. As painkillers and liquid sustenance fed into my head, the waste would come in a steady trickle down the tube emanating from my bladder and down my pyjama trouser leg. I still hallucinated every night and day, but that was getting less severe.

In the dead of night I felt a grinding pain in my abdomen. It seemed as though I was dying. I thrashed about in the clutches of my agony. With not an inkling of what it could be I rang the bell and the nurse came hurrying in. He put hot wet towels on my stomach to stave off the cramps, all to no avail, and told me not to worry, that it was just trapped wind. After an hour, where I was seeing all manner of coloured patterns on the big screen of the inside of my eyelids, the pain dissipated.

The night staff had to turn me over whenever I rang the bell, which was about ten times a night. I became agitated and impatient if they didn't come straight away. It was only possible to lie on my left side or my back. I had to have a pillow between my knees, two pillows behind my back and one pillow to cushion my right arm, which lay out in front of me like a pauper I once saw on the pavement in Delhi begging for alms. An electric fan kept me cool, even though only a thin sheet covered me. A big Australian in the next bed asked the nurse to ask me if I could turn it off because he was chilled. Why he didn't ask me directly I don't know. I then proceeded to swelter and sweat my way through the long night. Just another long night of many.

I had some idea of what had happened to me now and I just kept breaking down in tears. Why me? Hadn't I been through enough these last five years? Two major accidents from which to convalesce, taking a year apiece, four illnesses, hepatitis, pericarditis, amoebic dysentery, and fatigue syndrome. I was weary and if I could I would have screamed out, 'amputate the damned legs, they're fucking useless to me now. I'm better off without them.'

If there'd been someone around with a saw I wouldn't have hesitated to have them lopped off. After all I couldn't feel a thing in them. In fact it was the opposite of the phantom limb phenomenon, where the leg or arm is amputated and for months, even years, after there is a ghostly feeling of the limb still in its place. The amputee will jump out of bed convinced that he has two legs and promptly fall over. My situation was the exact opposite. I could see I had the leg and the arm when I was looking at them, but when I averted my eyes they completely ceased to exist.

The last two accidents were my fault but this . . . I didn't even see it coming. I was aware of nothing. One minute I was jumaring, the next I was upside down on the end of the rope, trying to shrug my rucsac off my shoulders. One moment I was penduluming in a sweeping arc and fifteen minutes later coming round and wondering what all this blood was doing gushing from my head and staining the water crimson.

Lying there however I could now see how all three major accidents might be seen as subconsciously, subliminally self-inflicted. I had become bored with a pretty extreme lifestyle. What hope for me was there if I was disenchanted with doing just what I wanted, going right there to the edge of life and screaming, 'You can't touch me, you bastards!' I never had anyone telling me what to do, never had a career apart from climbing, never worked nine to five. Most people have a climbing career that spans perhaps ten years and the rest is steadily downhill. There are some notable exceptions to this but even they would agree that there was a decade when they achieved most. For the last three years I was doing what I thought I should be doing and not what I really wanted to do. By continuing to climb I wasn't learning anything new, wasn't breaking into higher levels of consciousness or know-ledge. So I knew something had to snap. I could feel it in my bones.

The first falling and drowning incident in Wen Zawn at Gogarth in '93 was because I was screwed up over a girl and thought she might notice me if I hurt myself. Let's put it this way, she was on my mind when I fell off, ripped all my gear and wiped out. It wasn't a conscious thought, but I'm sure it flashed across my mind.

The second, on Creagh Meaghaidh, in the Highlands of Scot-land, was because I was desperate to change my life. I fell 200 feet off an ice climb. I was tired of it all and I recall breathing a sigh of relief when I awoke in hospital. There was a huge release of pressure. No more climbing, no more routes, no more egos, no more grades, no more sponsors trying to tell me what to do, no more weight crushing down on me and saying, 'Excel!' Even if that pressure came from within. I didn't know what else to do at the time to find a replacement. That was the problem. So I drifted back onto the climbing treadmill. And so it all began over again.

I put myself in that situation purposefully but without knowing it at the time. I didn't wilfully throw myself off the ice but I wouldn't have got myself into that situation – soft eggshell ice, miles out from an ice screw – if I was thinking rationally.

And this latest and final accident was because I felt trapped. I had it all, or that's what the majority of my friends figured – big house with a beautiful garden, nice car, as many holidays as I would care to take. Happy at home with Celia. Basically, I was very comfortable. I was taking too many risks and I didn't know why. Why was I not wearing a helmet? If there's a rock climbing situation which warrants wearing a helmet it was surely then. Why didn't I glance up and see the rock coming? I normally would have been much more aware of my surroundings. The only conclusion I can come to is that I was stressed out by my relationship and by climbing also, but on a subconscious level, without really mentally coming to terms with what I was challenging in my lifestyle.

Try as I might, I couldn't get a crap out. The reason for this constipation was that I had such an energetic life before and now I was lying immobile in bed. Plus I was lying flat on my back with a bed pan under me, which isn't conducive to a good shit, especially if you are used to going in the woods, squatting. It was a week before my first shit and that wasn't without several false starts and enemas. When the pretty blonde nurse, Melissa, bunged my arse with an enema I felt every shred of self-dignity vaporise and, you know what, it didn't matter to me one little bit.

Nicola Mackinnon and Dawn Lewis were my physiotherapists and they were a light-hearted pair. The trick is to get you moving from day one or as near as damn it. First lesson would be sitting on the side of the bed, which may sound easy, but with hemiplegia it isn't. I toppled over to the right again and again until I learnt how to balance on my left buttock. Though I would often get caught unawares and occasionally overbalance for weeks to come.

Once I'd vaguely mastered how to sit upright, I was whisked off to the physio gym where there were all manner of torture implements. Parallel bars, blocks, rubber balls from three inches to three feet in diameter, tilt boards, cupboards full of every terrible thing, splints, casts and slings, items that were going to become as familiar as the hairs in the ditch in my head over the coming months.

There they had me rolling a big ball whilst sitting down, my good hand holding my bad hand down. I would move it side to side and backward and forwards. Next I would be taught how to turn over, completely rotating, while lying down. Simple movements have a habit of becoming fights in desperation with a 'dense hemi', as the doctors call my condition.

It was then that I saw that guy in the mirror at the end of the parallel bars. I didn't recognise the man in front of me. Half his face was black and blue and he had a haemorrhaged eyeball. I knew this term because I'd had one before when my ice axe hit me in the orbit around my eye during the 200-foot fall on Creagh Meaghaidh. His whole eyeball was a deep cherry red, as if he'd been using cochineal eye drops. He was thin beyond belief. With the shaved head he resembled a Jew in the black and white Pathe News film footage of the liberation of the concentration camps. I couldn't take my eyes off the man in the mirror as I couldn't take my eyes off that black and white film. His head was poorly shaved with long bits on the sides and he still had matted blood in it and falling off sticky tape on top. He also had a 'golden purse' with him, a catheter bag full of deep orange piss, which he hung on the parallel bars. That had to be emptied before every session but it soon filled up with the exercise.

Presently Marge Conroy the speech therapist tested me for swallowing ability. A kind, interested woman who had me sipping orange juice and eating ice cream by the teaspoon. I was then controlled for a number of days, eating little bits of easy to swallow food and tasting protein drink. Pretty soon I was being force fed, 'to get my weight up', three massive meals a day, plus five protein shakes. My dietician would come round and make sure I was eating and drinking all I should. Celia told them that I had always been this weight but they seemed not to believe her. How could anyone look this emaciated? They obviously had not seen other climbers I could mention.

I was complaining to the nurse, by pointing at my throat, about my naso-gastric tube and how it was choking me. Burnt chillies, that's what it was like. It was getting to the point where I couldn't even breathe any more without breaking into a coughing fit. Jane Boucher, a kind nurse, pulled it out because she felt sorry for me, but then faced stiff reprimands from the dietician who thought he was the one who should say whether it stayed or went. It was a momentous occasion. With the sliding out of that tube I suddenly felt free, the whole world was mine.

I preferred the chocolate to the banana milkshakes, but after a couple of days I got sick of the sight of either. I couldn't feed myself so well with my non-dominant hand. It would take more than an hour, lying down, and I would get most of the food down my front and onto the blue napkin. But it was bliss to be eating on my own rather than with the tube. My favourites were kidney bean casserole, followed by green jelly or ice cream. Celia brought me boxes of mixed bean salad in to ease my constipation but I still hadn't been for a week. I was on my third or fourth enema when I finally shat with great relief. They had been shovelling food into me all week and up till then nothing had come out the other end.

Marge's full title was speech and language therapist and she had me doing exercises with my mouth, making different shapes with it and saying 'aaaaah' or 'oooooh'. She also made me look at picture cards and asked me to say what they depicted. I stared long and hard at a picture of a pen and raised my hands in disbelief. Then a picture of a house brick. 'Don't know,' I struggled to utter. An elephant, a horse, a shovel, a book, all manner of items and animals. I recognised them but just could not think of their names.

'We've all forgotten someone's name now and again and it's just a profound version of that,' said Marge. 'Anomic asphasia it's called.'

My left from my right I persistently got confused and I had lost the actual concept of time. I couldn't say what clocks did. As the days passed, I found that I slowly came to understand, but there was still no way I could tell the time. So it was back to junior school for me with pictures of clocks and 'The big hand is pointing to the nine and the small hand is pointing towards the three. No, Paul, it's not five to six!'

Then she would test my mental processing power and speed.

'Name all the animals you can think of in the farmyard in a minute?' she asked in her soft Tassie lilt.

'Er, pig . . .' There was then a long pause until the minute was up.

'OK, this time I want you to think of as many words as you can beginning with the letter "C".'

I looked around the ward, hoping to cheat and there it was, as if in neon lights, 'Australia's no. 1 Catheter provider'. She knew what I was up to straight away. I recognised the C and then the rest of the word as I stuttered out, 'C-ath-et-er.' And my minute was up.

Pretty soon the telephone started ringing and hardly stopped – my mother, father, brother, friends. I couldn't talk to them, so had Celia put their fears to rest as best she could. Faxes came in a steady stream. Indeed, the Outside Shop in Llanberis had its own free fax service to me. In all I received seventy-five faxes and it was these that kept me going. Knowing that I was not forgotten while I was halfway around the world was crucial if I was to remain positive. And every fax that came was a piece of home and got pasted to the wall of the ward until you couldn't see the paintwork.

After about a week my voice began slowly to return, though I had no control over what came out of my mouth. Celia reminded me that the first word that she heard me utter was 'OK'. On the phone to Llanberis I told Gwion Hughes that 'One had to take one's leave for one had laundry to do.' That was a strange period for me, perhaps the strangest period. I had such a limited vocabulary that I couldn't construct sentences the way I wanted to. With the royal we or one it was much easier to say what I wanted to say (although I never had any laundry). When Noel Craine rang me up I told him, 'Not to worry for we would soon be having sex.' This was right there in front of Celia and it made us both break into hysterics. I wonder what Freud would have made of that one.

Celia was shocked to hear me ordering the staff about. It was as if I didn't know how to be polite and we joked about how my politeness lobe had been wiped out by the rock. I would only say 'Food' when I was hungry and 'Drink' when I was thirsty. I was desperately trying to do better, at Celia's insistence, and managed the odd time to get out 'Pass me food' or 'Shut the window.' That still wasn't polite enough for Celia and it is due to her and her wrist-slapping every time I slipped up that I have my current amount of politeness. Basically, I was slightly disinhibited but not to the same extent as some patients I would see during my journey through rehab. After only two weeks I was using please and thank you every time I wanted something.

The Dribble Queen, as the urologist is affectionately known in Australia, was assigned to me when I came off the catheter and suffered a retention of water in my bladder. My belly swelled up like a football and hurt me a great deal, yet, try as I might, I still couldn't piss. Steaming towels laid on my stomach and taps running to imitate the sound of urination were all to no avail. Five times I had to have the catheter re-inserted and in my mind the nurses seemed to be getting frustrated and angry with me. I'm sure that was just paranoia though.

The consultant considered putting a suprapubic catheter in. This gruesome device goes through the muscle of the abdomen and into the bladder wall. I tried extra hard to pee when I heard this discussed but I only succeeded in straining a muscle. Each time the catheter tube was threaded up into my bladder the relief I experienced was incredible. As I watched my belly deflating I could only picture a car tyre with a puncture. It is normal for someone to want to go and piss when they are carrying 350ml in their bladder. I was frequently carrying 1400ml in mine and it stretched the thing. Anyway the docs finally decided to leave a catheter in until I returned home, thereby palming the problem off onto someone else. And, let's face it, that was the least of my worries.

Pete Steane, who had challenged my pursuit of new routes, came in to see us about that time. He knew about survival of course and shared his anecdotes about lack of bladder control. About how he found it hard to get partners for his climbs because he couldn't get used to the leg bag and so did without. His partners had to endure a steady golden rain coming from up above as the offensive liquid trickled down his shorts leg. He always carries a bicycle pump around with him and one day I asked him why. He self-catheterises whenever his bladder gets full and the bicycle pump holder is just the perfect length to fit the tube in. Self-catheterisation is something with which I was going to become very familiar during my time in Bangor.

Celia asked the doctor whether she could take me outside for half an hour and he agreed, as long as she promised to have me back for lunch. To get out into the big wide world we had to negotiate a corridor that went on for at least a mile with one particular photograph in it of a child burn victim. I remember he was bandaged from the neck down and appeared to be doing physiotherapy in some form. He looked incongruous because he was laughing and I would have expected him to look miserable. That is until I became crippled. I now felt ecstatically and unex-plainably happy. Perhaps it was the thrill of having survived a near fatal accident that the boy and I had in common. Celia and I had to descend a floor by lift, cross a foyer, and then we were out.

I'd been out of intensive care for about a week and the bruising on my face, and red eye was still very apparent. This I could tell by the horrified stares that some of the passers by were giving me. Obviously at that time I hadn't developed a strategy for putting them off, like staring back at them until they got the gist. I just felt embarrassed for my looks.

It was unbearably bright so we went straight to Salamanca, the local market, to buy sunglasses. I bought a pair of five-dollar shades and soaked up the atmosphere. There were people everywhere crowding the street. When I heard 'El Condor Pasa' played by an authentic South American pipe band the tears rolled down my face. I asked Celia for a dollar and threw it in the hat. The hustle and bustle put the life that had been missing back into me. I know it sounds clichéd but that market woke me up and made me want to live again. Before I was an over-emotional being, crying all the time but with no feeling. Not sad nor happy, not depressed nor suicidal, but confused and labile.

We sat at a table on the pavement where we had arranged to meet Sue Duff who had taken us under her wing and cared for us a great deal. Chris Bonington had put her on to us when he heard of our predicament and we couldn't have been more grateful. I instantly warmed to her as she came into the hospital ward with her essential oils and tonics for the brain and a small cylindrical pillow for my whiplashed neck. She also brought in a little bean bag to shut out the light from my over-sensitive eyes and a relaxation CD which I had trouble listening to. Celia had gone out and brought me the compact disc player and lots of Shostakovich and Sibelius but I was finding music hard going. It just sounded like noise at first. Had I lost my appreciation of music? This really saddened me. Would it ever come back?

Sue is a guide in Tibet. She takes people around Mount Kailas when she is working and was also in the process of building a new timber frame house. Later she would take us into her home and give us tea and cake. Then we would go through to her bedroom and Celia and I would lie in her bed and receive visualisation therapy from her. Amidst the many Buddhas, including one given to her by His Holiness the Dalai Lama, I fell asleep. When I awoke Celia was accepting a relaxation massage from Sue because, 'She had undergone a trauma as well, you know!'

They drank coffee and I orange juice, all the while under the penetrating stares of passers by, and so we went to see the fishing boats and yachts. They took it in turns to push me along the pavement and found that the streets of Hobart were not designed for wheelchair-users or their pushers. Sometimes pavements could be a foot high with no ramps onto or off them. Being under the ozone hole the sun had an intensity about it that was ferocious and I had to smother my face in sunblock, so I looked shockingly pale. I especially had to hide my head wound under a hat. I expect I might have looked like Frankenstein's monster with thirty staples in my shaven head without it. I would certainly have attracted even more attention to myself.

We stopped at an ice cream shop and I can still taste the pistachio, six months afterwards. I looked at my reflection in the ice cream shop window and thought that I looked like the guy out of *Natural Born Killers* with my new shades on. Celia joked, 'More like Stevie Wonder.' I recall the lobster pots piled on the quayside, woven together using willow, so intricately. I recall fishing vessels of all colours, shapes and sizes, ghostly quiet and gently bobbing on the swell, not a soul in sight. I recall feasting on fish and chips bought from a boat, not giving a second thought about being back in the hospital for lunch, and polishing off the lot. I recall the clinking-clanking of the yachts' rigging on the masts and out in the harbour, dinghies racing. And I recall that smell of fish and seaweed that only comes from harbours with their piles of nets on the quayside. I can smell it still, now. And then, all too soon, it was time to go back, past the skate boarder and through the doors into the stupefying atmosphere of the hospital.

Marge, my speech therapist, came every day, as did all my other therapists, including Rebecca, my occupational therapist. She showed me how to put my shirt on whilst supporting my arm, which didn't hurt because there was no feeling in it, but which was quite obviously dislocated. She taught me how to put my trousers on with only one arm by crossing my affected leg over my good leg so that my foot was suspended. Then I could pull the trouser leg up my own leg. She also brought me slings for in the shower or bath and slings for out, and non-slip matting which was going to keep my plate still while I was eating, instead of it running away with me like a glass on an ouija board.

My favourite part of the day was seven o'clock in the morning, shower time. The nurses soon went from giving me bed baths to taking me for a shower, to get me up in a wheelchair as quickly as possible. It is imperative that they establish a degree of independence straight away. Melissa or Richard would put my arm in the sling, to stop it subluxing (dislocating), and wheel me in on a plastic shower chair. The day's sweat would come washing off me under the hot jet as I was helped with difficult bits. Sometimes I could have a bath, which involved an electric hoist coming onto the ward, a bit like one of those cranes you see changing street light bulbs. I would shove over in my bed until I was on the platform and then be wheeled through reception to the bathroom. There I'd be lowered into a waiting bath of barely tolerable water with a sharp intake of breath.

We had another visitor about this time – my rescuer, Neale Smith, the only paramedic with any climbing experience. He told me the story of how it was too difficult for the helicopter to land and so it dropped him and Sergeant Paul Steane (Pete's brother – it's a small world in Tasmania) off in the undergrowth, how he tackled the Tyrolean rope traverse and abseiled to one of the two New South Waleans and me (the other of the pair was on the mainland and on hand to give any assistance). Neale had the kindest face you can imagine, consoling eyes, and a soft Australian voice. He told me of how Hobart had been his home all his life, of his beachside house, of his family troubles and his little boy. He reckoned I was lucky that he was on duty because he usually goes out with his son to some pretty wild places. And even though he would have been on call he probably wouldn't have got to the Tote before dark.

Celia's sister Elaine flew all the way out from England because she knew her little sis was in distress. It was very strange seeing her walk through that door. We hugged a hug as firmly as I could muster. She cried and I cried. She brought me a personal cassette player, which I could just about tolerate by now, and two copies of my first book. I remember signing a copy for Neale, the first of many signed left-handed, and it being illegible.

Later Phil, my oldest and dearest friend, flew in all the way from the UK, too. OK, so he was in Australia for work purposes anyway, but I was touched how he cared. He didn't have to come all the way down to Tasmania. I thought that I'd dreamt about making the arrangement with him so that when he walked onto the ward I was convinced that I was hallucinating again. He brought mail and warm wishes from old Lancashire friends, some of whom I hadn't seen in a decade. He was generally like a breath of fresh air and always had a smile for us.

Nerves were getting frayed between Celia and myself. When I tried to explain to her that Nurse Moy had tried to kill me she hit the roof. The words burst forth out of my mouth in a splutter, just like they always did when I was attempting to speak. 'Nurse Moy tried to murder me,' I shouted stiltedly. Celia began weeping and then I saw out of my right eye that Nurse Moy was actually in the room. Celia stormed out of the ward scarlet with embarrassment whilst I was left to stew in my own juice, still terrified of Moy. I was confused to say the least. For two weeks I had been trying to hold this event in my memory, forgetting it completely and then desperately struggling to recall it. As soon as I thought I could say the words, they just came splurging out. As far as I was concerned it was totally true; she had tried to kill me. It was more than paranoia; my own grey matter had deluded me.

Nicola cried out, 'I saw a flicker.'

'Where?' I asked excitedly.

'In your quad. Your thigh muscle I mean,' she corrected herself to simplify it for me.

We were in the neuro-gym, between the parallel bars. I was stepping up on to a box, which basically involved Nick lifting my leg up for me and placing my foot on the box. It was a highly emotional moment and I couldn't contain myself, even if I hadn't actually seen it. I thought that my leg would never work again and then, right there, was this glimmer of hope. I was going to have these moments again and again, where I had been trying for a certain movement for so long that I never thought it would come. And then, all of a sudden . . . I got quite blasé about them later but not now. The tears welled up and rolled down my face. Nick, who was kneeling before me controlling my knees, said with water in her eyes, 'If you don't stop it I'm going to start crying too.' I went back to my room completely made up and couldn't wait to tell Celia the good news.

Later, as I lay in my bed, the speech therapist came on her daily visit. Marge asked, 'What is five plus seven?' After a pause that seemed to go on forever I retorted that I hadn't a clue.

'Twelve,' she said disappointedly, 'is the answer. Let's make this a little easier for you. Can you tell me the answer to one plus two?'

After an interval of a full five minutes I thought I had the answer. 'Five,' I exclaimed proudly.

She answered 'Nooo, three,' in a sympathetic tone. She then went on to explain how 'dyscalculia, that's the high-flying term us therapists give to difficulties in performing mathematical operations, is a common symptom of an injury to the left hemisphere of the brain.' That I shouldn't worry because, 'These things have a habit of settling down in their own time.'

There was a Canadian guy who had had a tumour removed from his brain asleep in the next bed. I liked him. He was sociable. In fact I only met one patient, nurse or doctor who wasn't extremely sociable and she had lost her long and short term memory in a car smash. They went into the Canadian's brain through his nose, which had been bandaged with a big pad of wadding which was seeping blood. He was ordered not to sneeze or blow his nose, as there was a hole directly into his brain. If he sneezed I supposed his brains would fall out of his nostrils. There was this hauntingly beautiful girl who kept walking past the ward door every five minutes invariably followed by a nurse who tried to coax her back into bed. She had no memory and didn't even know her mother and father's names. I remember pondering in my confused state on the unbearableness of it all for them, and thinking, her life isn't worth living any more. Everytime she woke she didn't know where she was or how long she had been there. She was only sixteen. I later thanked my lucky stars that I only had hemiplegia and that I had most of my memory intact, a problem of the motor cortex instead of anything cognitive. During my voyage through rehab these thoughts would change radically.

I was slowly coming to terms with the fact that I may never go climbing again. This realisation was aided by Dr Khan's insistence that I would never be able to walk again, never mind climb. He looked a bit like a hare and had a little paunch squeezed into his expensive silk suit. 'Just think yourself lucky that you still have one arm and one leg. Some persons have only their mouth that is usable.' His remark made my heart sink and I began weeping. He came from Peshawar, near the Afghanistan border, and I wondered if he had grown up in a crueller environment than I had – a rocket launcher can be bought over the counter in Peshawar.

Once a day all the doctors and surgeons would come on a ward round. It could be any time. There was Mr Van Gelder, my personal surgeon, Dr Khan, Dr Liddell and the ward sister whose name I forget. They would all hover round the foot of the bed and make notes on their clipboards: 'suprapubic catheter', or 'nasogastric feed out'. I would stammer out my hello before any of them had a chance to beat me to it and they would, without fail, read my new faxes that I had received overnight. Some of them were very funny indeed. George Smith, a close friend from Wales, sent me numerous cartoons he had drawn with expertise and there were all manner of paintings and cards arriving all the time. And so they would all troop out in a line just as quickly as they had entered, muttering to each other under their breath.

Van Gelder wore round spectacles, had a square jaw and the air of a Thunderbird about him. He was a climber himself, a damn fine one. He had climbed a couple of 8000-metre peaks, including

Kangchenchunga in Sikkim, and Broad Peak in Pakistan. He was on K2 in 1986 when Julie Tullis and Al Rouse died in a ferocious storm. He knew his stuff, that is for sure, but he gave all that up to become a neuro-surgeon, finding he could get the same kicks without the risk to his own life. That out-of-body experience which you search for all your climbing life and only pick up about five times during your whole career, he now finds in surgery. He described looking down on himself at work just as a climber does when she or he is having one of those rare 'special moments', usually in a very scary situation. He also thought that he could do more good saving people's lives than in the selfish act that is mountain climbing. Undeniably, I was indebted to him for having saved my life. He quietly voiced the opinion that, 'There is too much senseless wasting of lives in climbing. I had to get out before it got me.' I liked to think he took a little extra care because he knew we shared a love of the mountains, but I know that he uses the same expertise with all his patients.

He was interested in the use of helmets in climbing and discussed helmet design in great detail with Celia. He ruminated on the notion that I could have been in a worse state had I been wearing a helmet. Many motorcycle accidents result in quadraplegia because, when a smash happens, the motorcyclist breaks his cervical spine, whereas if he wasn't wearing a helmet he would have a head injury – the same as me. Obviously neither option is particularly appealing but at least I was 'just' a hemiplegic. At least I had one good arm and one good leg. Had I been wearing a helmet maybe I would have been quadrapleged also.

Celia came onto the ward in the night-time. She was distraught and weeping. What could be troubling her? She had been allowed to sleep in a little room that the hospital staff use for such cases as ourselves, people from foreign lands who have had grim accidents. It turned out that someone had shouted at her while she was asleep and when she awoke, startled, they were gone. When daylight came it proved to be a simple case of double-booking and when the worried, sleep-deprived relative of the other patient looked in and saw Celia asleep she lost her temper.

The nurses pleaded with Celia to stay but she thought it would be better for all if she moved out. Nurse Jane Boucher was fast becoming a close friend of Celia's by now, having taken a lost waif under her wing; she even ended up buying the Falcon because Celia was desperate to get shot of it. Now she kindly offered to let Celia stay with her. One evening we went to dinner at Jane's house. She cooked everything vegan and I, having been on an ice cream diet for two weeks, just shovelled anything into my mouth. We laughed when I commented, with my mouth full of cream, 'Oh, I was vegan.'

Soon afterwards we took a drive up Mount Wellington. Since Nick, my physio, had taken me to the hospital car park and shown me how to transfer from my wheelchair in and out of the car, there was no stopping me. I just had to take extra care to protect my head from the smacking against the doorframe. Up the switchbacks we motored until we reached the Organ Pipes. I asked Celia to stop and gazed mournfully up at what I knew I had lost.

It wasn't just the physical act of climbing a rock but the whole event: the crack with your mates before you tie into the rope, before you put on your serious cap; in the pub afterwards (where a good day's climbing invariably ends) discussing this move or that move; wild nights that you felt entitled to because you had burnt up so much energy during the day. And then there was the travelling which meant so much to me. I felt that I would rather die than not be able to go on expeditions ever again. Fifteen years of my life I had spent going on expeditions or 'trips' as we called them, more or less back to back. I had witnessed flying saucer clouds from halfway up a wall in Patagonia, a plume of dust rising for thousands of feet during a gigantic rockfall, seen from the top of a mountain in Kirghizstan. And all of them watched, in awe, with special friends. I buried such memories and told Celia to drive on.

When we arrived at the summit of the mountain I transferred into my chair and took deep draughts of the rarefied air at 4000 feet. We wheeled down a plank-walk to the viewing gantry from where we could survey the whole of the Derwent estuary, its harbour and the city of Hobart. I could see the hospital from up here, model-like, and the Tasman Bridge, so clear was the atmosphere. It was a moving experience to be looking down upon the land and sea again instead of staring up at the ceiling from my hospital bed. To the west the Atlantic Ocean disappeared over the horizon, unchecked, as at 40° South, it peaked and troughed its way a clear half around the globe. In my over-emotional state I shed a tear at the vastness of the world.

Roxanne Wells and Chris Piesker came in to see us. They were scheduled to be filming on the Totem Pole the very next day after the accident. It was an all-star cast that also included Steve Monks and Enga Lokey, whom we had met walking in, rigging the stack with ropes for the various camera angles. We had ruined their plans because the rescue team had dropped the Tyrolean rope traverse, which meant they had to get the rope back over there before they could start the filming. They had to spend the day re-climbing the Tote, which they did and got some excellent footage by all accounts. Chris wasn't just in the hospital to visit me. He also had an accident, a severe compound fracture to his middle finger that needed pinning. It too had been caused by a falling rock. Both of them were of a typical climber build, lean and muscular, and he wore as much jewellery as she did. When they departed I remember him holding my head up, as though it were a chalice, and kissing me on the forehead.

Greg the parson offered to pray for me and I accepted. That was the first time I had ever asked for prayer. Perhaps it was his soothing manner or the fact that I believe in the power of prayer because hundreds of folk putting their hands together must have some positive effect. Perhaps I have belief buried deep down inside me or maybe it is just conditioning. But tell me of the person who isn't going to ask God for forgiveness on his deathbed. OK, so I'd come through the worst of it and knew that I wasn't going to die (not unless I had a haemorrhage or a fatal seizure) but as far as I could make out I would be a severe cripple from now on. I've heard that virtually everyone asks God for forgiveness when dying, even if they're non-believers, 'just in case'.

Celia was busy finding out when we were to leave the hospital and be repatriated. We had been there nearly three weeks now and she was convinced they were telling us cock and bull stories to delay us.

'He has to be in a stable condition,' Dr Khan kept reiterating. 'Who knows what effect going up in a plane will have? The cabin is pressurised to 10,000 feet and that is a hell of a lot.' He was correct, it had to be said. I didn't want any complications like a burst head if I could help it. Imagine the pressure differential between the inside of your head and at 10,000 feet.

Having the staples removed from my head was OK, or so I thought. Then the nurse hit a particularly difficult one to extract and began twisting the pliers into my skull while I broke out in a sweat and gritted my teeth. It was a job that needed doing before I could fly anywhere. There were only three staples that were hard and painful to get out. And she told me encouragingly, 'The head has less pain receptors than anywhere else on the skin's surface.' Now I have all thirty of them in a little glass jar waiting to be melted down and made into a pendant or earring.

There was a date being bandied around, the 8th March. I did not believe that we would leave then, it seemed too good to be true. All I wanted, more than anything, was to see my friends and family back home. I had given them the shock of their lives and they had responded with a barrage of beautiful words, whether it be by fax or letter or sometimes painted.

'As well as long-term physiotherapy,' Mr Van Gelder advised, 'I can only recommend the support of your family and friends.'

Because of all the letters and faxes I had received I knew that I could count on them. He also mentioned, 'When your head settles down, perhaps in a couple of years, you could have cranioplasty, a plate fitted in your skull.'

These are some notes from the discharge letter to the consultant who would be taking me on back in the UK:

This 30 years old patient was admitted on 13th February 1998 after head injury. He was a rock climber who was hit in the head accidentally with a rock. He had no helmet.

Neurological examination on 16/02/98: Right-sided hemiplegia, severe expressive dysphasia.

During his stay on the ward, the physiotherapist, speech therapist and occupational therapist treated the patient. Occasionally patient needs reinsertion of his IDC. Bladder function remains one of the problems. On the 28/02/98 speech pathologist report showed that mild/moderate anomic-asphasia [inability to name objects] was resolved, but dysgraphia [inability to understand the concept of writing], dyscalculia [inability to do simple arithmetic], right/left confusion, finger agnosia [inability to name your fingers on either hand] and mild visuospatial difficulties [missing a cup when you reach out for it] were present. Cognitive function is largely preserved.

The physiotherapist noted some improvement in right lower limb function, including some muscle power in pelvic muscles.

Hepatitis B (surface) Antigen: NOT DETECTED, Hepatitis A Antibodies: NOT DETECTED.

HIV EIA: NOT DETECTED.

On discharge from hospital, the patient is in a stable condition, and able for the air transport home.

6

RETURNED EMPTY

There is no returning game between a man and his stars.

Samuel Beckett,
Murphy

She was not at all what one would have expected of a Scottish doctor. An old matronly woman or middle-aged professional man perhaps. But not an oddly attractive six foot Amazon, squeezed into a black mini skirt, with make-up by the shovel full, breasts held firmly in place with a Wonder Bra under a tight red tee-shirt. This willowy glamorous doctor entered the ward with the look of Betty Boop about her. She was to be my escort for the flight home. She carried the scent of jonquils, that springtime smell, and was from Edinburgh. You could tell this by her guttural, while at the same time mellifluous and caring accent. Her name was Susan.

All the nurses and therapists huddled together for a photograph. It makes me warm in my heart to look at those pictures now. All those smiling faces. Moy and Jenny whom I kept confusing, Herbert the Swiss who cycled to hospital every day, blonde Melissa, Richard with his ponytail, Ian who once bought three kilos of chocolate because it was on sale, Jane who competed in the Cradle to Coast Race. I can only recall the faces of the others who did just as good a job; it's just my impaired memory that makes me forget some names.

We were to be driven to the airport by Neale the climbing paramedic, to whom I'd already said my emotional farewells. He pushed a stretcher trolley into the room where Celia was busy taking down all the faxes. As I was strapped in I took one last look around me at the now bare room. It held some good and some painful memories that room. The constant headache for the first week was a bad memory but my mate Phil and Celia's sister Elaine turning up out of the blue from England and the cheerful, accommodating faces of the nursing staff were good ones.

I was wheeled outside in the stretcher, much to my annoyance. Why I couldn't use a chair I didn't know. The chill air bit into my clean-shaven face as I was shoved in the back of the wagon. Susan and Neale sat with me in the ambulance, which careered round bends with me all strapped down.

We were soon at the airport and I posed self-consciously, for photos with the back doors of the ambulance open. I was wearing my raggedy baseball cap and now when I look at those photographs I see a haunted, gaunt face staring back at me, trying to smile. Phil helped Celia weigh our numerous hefty bags whilst I reclined in the ambulance. Jane arrived to say farewell and I gave Phil a goodbye hug with one arm, which felt awkward and stupid.

We bypassed officialdom and drove straight onto the runway. A truck with a lift, a kind of cherry-picker affair, came to meet us and I was wheeled from one vehicle to the other. It is a small runway at Hobart with just a handful of aeroplanes on domestic flights; ours was bound for Melbourne. As the truck reversed up to the plane, the noise of the jet engines worried me. It started to lift and when the box was level with the jet a door opened and I was pulled in. The cabin was empty, apart from the few stewards hanging around, waiting to be useful. I was handled roughly into a wheelchair by so-called trained paramedics and pushed down the aisle to my stretcher. This wasn't as wide as I would have liked. In fact it was so damned narrow I only had room to lie flat on my back. I hoped that the following thirty hours to London would be more comfortable.

No sooner had we taken off, than we were flying over the Bass Strait and touching down at Melbourne. When we did Susan realised that my catheter bag was full to bursting. It must have been an effect of the change of pressure on my bladder.

The same procedure as loading me on was followed in reverse on disembarkation. We were wheeled to a sick bay with no coffee but at least I could sit up and psyche the scene for two hours before the next seven-hour leg to Singapore.

There were eleven seats booked on the insurance: one for the doctor, one for the nurse, one for Celia and eight for me. I was loaded up again, first on, and strapped down in a harness affair that parachutists use with an extra strap for good measure around the thighs. I was supposed to wear this all through the flight but the thought of ditching into the Sea of Timor off Sumatra and still being strapped in to a stretcher was too terrifying, so I persuaded my Scottish doctor to take it off. This was until I fell off my stretcher, and went crashing down into the seats below, because it was much too narrow.

The curtain was supposed to give me some privacy but I insisted on having it open so I could see what was going on. Celia said, 'I bet people are jealous that you're lying down, in repose, while they have to sit in cramped seats.' But I knew better and grew paranoid that they were staring at me because of my looks. The bruising had virtually disappeared from my face but I still sported a skinhead with a sticker on the top advising 'HANDLE WITH CARE: BONY DEFECT', and a bright, glowing red 'Terminator' eyeball. All the passengers could tell I was in a mess and the falling off my stretcher incident didn't help my appearance either. Anybody that made eye contact with me I scowled at with all the vehemence my happy-go-lucky nature could muster.

I was turned the other way from the telly so I was the only one of 400 people who couldn't see the thing. This I wouldn't have minded but there are times when even the most patient patient gets bored during a long-haul flight. Alan, the nurse, kept a careful eye on me, monitoring my pill intake, that is feeding me two paracetamol every four hours, and making sure to empty my catheter bag. He was especially careful about protecting my head, which was still very squishy and vulnerable on top. At that time it wouldn't have taken a very large blow to the head to put it into trauma again.

All I remember about Singapore airport, besides the heat, was that it had Damon Hill's Formula One racing car in the transit lounge on a revolving podium. The Melbourne Formula One race had just taken place and all the drivers were in first class. Stewardesses were chatting excitedly about their famous cargo. Names I'd never heard of were rippling in whispers up and down the cabin.

It was heaven to get upright in a chair again, even if it was only for a couple of hours. Pretty soon it was time to get back on the merry-go-round of ambulances and lifts and stretchers and wheelchairs again for the ten-hour leg to London. Alan returned home to Australia and was replaced by an ageing English woman called Dora. She was as heavily made up as Susan and when they both stood over me, and stared intensely down, just checking everything was all right, I was reminded of the phantom masks one finds in Bolivia and Peru.

I swallowed two paracetamol and attempted to sleep but the pain in my neck was too great. At least they cured my throbbing headache. Thirty-five hours after leaving Tasmania we touched down at Heathrow where it was cloudy and fine, if colder than I would have liked. We were to be driven by ambulance the five hours to Wales. After a wait in the sickbay, where I was given hot sweet tea, I was wheeled back out into the biting cold and what I saw next appalled me. It wasn't the type of ambulance I was anticipating, no mini bus, but an estate car or station wagon with Celia busily squeezing haul bags into the back of it. I was too tired to kick up a fuss. I was squashed in the back, along with several haul bags and a peroxide blonde nurse who sat beside me the whole journey.

With her lippy and eyeliner she not only looked like a Barbie doll, but her name proved to be Barbie, too. Yet this outrageously artificial-looking woman spent her time raising money so that she could go to Bombay and distribute presents to orphans. Celia took her address and promised to send her some old rupees we had spare from our last trip there. She talked of the children with a genuine warmth and it was difficult to picture her, so clean and sentimental, in the filthy gutters of Bombay. Apparently the TV had already made one film documentary of her work there and were going to do a sequel as soon as she could raise the funds.

Wales was as beautiful as ever and spring was all around us. At the risk of over-quoting Beckett: 'What sky! What light! Ah in spite of all it is a blessed thing to be alive in such weather, and out of hospital.' Wonderfully familiar landmarks passed us by: the Marble Church, the Great Orme and the castle at Conwy. There was snow on the whale's back of Carnedd Llewelyn and the millions of daffodils on the central reservation past Llanfairfechan were in full bloom, a yellow ocean. After what felt like an eternity in hell we had finally made it home. Well, to Ysbyty Gwynedd, the hospital in Bangor.

It was said of colonial bishops who had come home from their dioceses that they had 'returned empty'. This description struck a chord with me. I could well be a bishop coming back from Tasmania, drained to the bottom.

7

BANGOR

---

*My cocoon becomes less oppressive, and my mind takes flight
like a butterfly. There is so much to do. You can wander off
in space or in time, set out for Tierra del Fuego or for king
Midas's court.*

*You can visit the woman you love, slide down beside her
and stroke her still-sleeping face. You can build castles in
Spain, steal the Golden Fleece, discover Atlantis, realise your
childhood dreams and your adult ambitions.*

Jean-Dominique Bauby,
The Diving-bell and the Butterfly

We arrived at Ysbyty Gwynedd and were brought through the
back door to a tiny cell looking out on a brick wall only a foot
or so from the window. We sat on an unmade bed, in Bueno
Ward, with no pillows and were ignored while the nurses attended
to more urgent business. The room was dirty and, though I had
a private toilet, that was filthy, too. The nurses were run off their
feet and had no time for mopping up the piss when my catheter
bag burst or even bringing me a cup of tea.

I reflected on the state of NHS hospitals in this country and on
how long a way we were from the Royal Hobart Hospital in both
distance and quality. A male nurse came and gave me a wet shave
with an old Bick razor. He was in such a rush to get it over and
done with he plucked most of the hairs clean out and I was left
with a bleeding rashed neck. He missed clumps too, so I felt like
a plucked chicken.

Visitors keen to see us instantly besieged us. David my brother came immediately from Ireland to visit. He looked handsome as ever and a little lighter than in his weight-lifting days. I had rarely seen him since we were kids. He used to take me and Judd, my mate from school, to the gym in his clapped out blue Bedford van. We used to train really hard but without proper coaching. I would swell with pride in front of Judd when my big brother won competitions. I used to love the smell of sweat on him. I could never sweat like that, but I was into all that iron and strapping, the stairway up into the top floor of the old mill, the swinging doors, the smell of old carpets, sweat and athlete's chalk.

All the memories of a childhood came back to me – Dave night-fishing with all his high-tech gear, the isotope floats, the quiver tips and swim-feeders. He was a good fisherman and won plenty of matches. He would cast his eight-ounce line into the reeds in the dead of night and always pull out a tench or carp. But piking was our favourite game. We would all head up to Killington Lake in Cumberland, in a VW Dormobile, with my dad and a bunch of his mates. Tents would be set up and we would cook the pike we had caught on an open fire. We used live bait, roach, so the bung would get towed all over the place for what seemed like ages and, suddenly, disappear. The excitement of playing a big pike in is incomparable. You strike hard and can feel, there's no question, if you have it or not. It plays dead until you've almost got it to the bank and then, just at that moment when its eyes meet yours, it turns and runs. The ratchet screams out and you fight to keep the fish under control. Too much tension and the line will snap, too little and the fish will run all your line out. This happens again and again until you have tired the pike out, and all that's left is to net the thing and disgorge the treble hook. They have the fiercest teeth of all coarse fish; concentric rows of needles all pointing inwards. You need to take great care not to skin the flesh off your fingers as you struggle to get the hook out.

I remember having a recurring fishing dream about this time, that I was doing just this. That I was using both my hands, oh so dextrously, tying on the treble hook and pushing it through the roach's dorsal fin. I was casting the line out with the index finger of my right hand and watching the bung bobbing around; striking, not too hard and not too light; playing the fish by reeling the line in with my right hand also. I am feeling the power of the fish as it runs out 300-odd feet of line; using the landing net to get the pike onto the bank and then disgorging the hook, carefully . . . carefully, with my right hand so as not to skin my knuckles.

When Dave left to get his ferry we both wept uncontrollably, just as if we were children again. Through the weeping my brother told me, 'You gave us a real fright, you know. We seriously thought you were dead.'

I promised never to put my family through that again, but they were hollow words somehow. I didn't know what the future held for me now; it was all up in the air. All I knew was that I couldn't know anything. According to the doctors all brain injuries are different, no two are the same, so looking at case histories would do no good.

At times not all the visitors could fit in the little room. At one point there were fifteen visitors which made me really tired and confused in conversation. It felt good to know I had so many friends but it was an exhausting time.

It was an emotional meeting with my mother for the first time since the accident. We had talked on the phone but judging by the sound of me, she expected I would be looking a lot worse. She said, as I have heard time after time, that she had never seen me looking so well. The five protein drinks I had been supping daily, since I had got rid of the naso-gastric tube, plus the three meals were all carefully monitored by the dietician. I had put on a stone in weight and was heavier than I ever had been. My face had lost virtually all its bruising, apart from a slight touch of rouge on the cheekbone and a patch of red on the white of the eyeball.

It wasn't that I dieted down to preserve my weight to be a climber. I was a vegetarian and I guess I ate healthily. Now my usually gaunt face had fattened out and so had my middle, which I became very self-conscious about. At six foot and weighing in at ten and a half stone you could say that I was a bit of a beanpole. I wouldn't say that I had a washboard stomach, but I did have some muscular definition. Now there was none, just puppy smooth fat.

My mum cried and gave me a big hug. She and my dad were the only ones who didn't want to know about the accident. It was refreshing not to have to talk about it. It was as if they instinctively knew that I was tired of it all and if I needed to rest I could do so without feeling guilty. It took me a few months to be able to say, 'No, I don't want to talk about it' to the many naturally inquisitive people.

I was in quarantine because I'd come from another hospital and might just be carrying that scourge of all hospitals, MRSA (Multi-Resistant Staphlacochus Aureus). The nurse came in and asked my friends politely to leave. She stuck a cotton bud right up my nose, under my armpit and inside my groin. To be used for swabs, she said. It's an infection that predominantly old people get, after hip replacement operations and things like that, and it is furiously resistant to antibiotics. Only two can treat it and if you use them without first making sure you've got the MRSA infection, you've effectively burnt your bridges.

After a week in quarantine, which was a joke because all and sundry were walking in and out of that door, and I would even be allowed out to the canteen and to physio, I was released. I was moved from the bowels of the hospital up to the immensely bright and cheerful Prysor Ward. It was good to get into the land of the living again. I'm a sociable man by nature and longed for company. There were six other men on Prysor.

There was Doug with his bionic arm, a strange device that he fitted every hour and it mechanically moved his arm for him. Then there was Mark who'd fallen off scaffolding straight through a conservatory. His feet were bruised to all hell and he couldn't stand on them, so he had to keep lying down. There was a very funny Cockney, Diamond Geezer, we called him, who had fallen down a flight of concrete stairs. He liked to have a joke and kept asking the nurses when the eggs and rashers were coming. Only the abnormally skinny and enfeebled would get a full breakfast and that only applied to just one person on the whole ward, who was isolated with the dreaded MRSA infection. This was Bernard who kept throwing his full set up and Diamond Geezer thought this a dreadful waste. Bernard was just across the corridor, so we could hear it all, every last heave. It sounded like somebody drowning. All Diamond could say was, 'It's a shame to blow 'em.'

Everybody was overweight on Prysor Ward and I mean well overweight. I dreaded night closing in because night-time was the domain of the snorers. One snorer you could say was normal, two unlucky, but five snorers on a ward of six was downright unimaginable. It was like trying to get a night's sleep amidst a herd of buffalo. Well, I don't know whether buffalo would make that much noise. Perhaps a pneumatic drill to the one side and a generator to the other would be more a fitting comparison to our cacophony of alto whistles and baritone growls. I was off all drugs now except anti-convulsants and I would plead with the nurses to dose me with some sleepers so I could get some shut-eye. The nurses refused to listen.

After a full six weeks without an erection I was thinking that I had lost my ability to have sex. Celia had asked Mr Van Gelder in Tasmania whether I would ever be able to have a family and the answer was that, as far as he knew, yes, he would. She didn't say anything to me, preferring that I raise the issue. But I was too frightened to hear a negative answer and so let it go in a swamp of worry. I was still worrying six weeks later when, one night, I had a wet dream. When I awoke from my fantasy it was the dead of night and I was still in the land of the dreaded snorers. But I couldn't contain my excitement, telling the night nurses and friends that came to visit the next day. I felt human again. Apparently it is the trauma of a severe head injury that is responsible for penile dysfunction and it usually rights itself after a few weeks. So I need not have gone through all that stress.

The view of the mountains from Prysor Ward was wondrous after staring at a brick wall for a week. You can see all fourteen peaks above 3000 feet from the ward window. The Carneddau, the Glyderau, including Tryfan and finally Yr Wyddfa, the highest mountain in Eryri and so in Wales. It has to be the best view of any hospital in the British Isles and it cheered me up no end. I would spend hours staring at that view from my wheelchair and wishing, just wishing. Tracing routes up the mountain ridges, I would go running along their tops and scrambling up their scree-covered slopes, diving into cold lakes and climbing gullies in the last remnants of the snow.

Friends would come visiting and I would strive to concentrate. Johnny Dawes came to see me and said, with a grin, 'You'll just have to start climbing one-handed. I'm doing 6a one-handed now.'

'How about one-handed and one-legged?' I replied.

As friends came in to visit me in hospital, I tried to remember the last time that I spent time with them prior to my accident. It was a way I could test my memory, but more often than not I had forgotten those moments completely: Trish, with a 'Hi' from behind the counter in Pete's Eats Cafe; Merlin, at home in Cae Canol, expounding some theory or other; Charlie with her velvet flares on Llanberis high street; Manuel with a goodbye hug for us on our round the world trip; having dinner with Anna and George and the kids the evening before we left; Noel and his ever so slightly envious expression as he shook farewell; Ali with her generous kisses and 'Ta-ra's'.

Gwyneth, the hospital urinologist, came in and, taking one look at my golden purse, declared, 'We'll have to get rid of that thing, won't we?' She explained in detail how I should go about self-catheterising myself and then told me to repeat her instructions, just in case I had missed anything. Then she handed me a clutch of straws and a tube of KY jelly. The nurse came in and removed my catheter and I was left to wait in nervous anticipation.

Dave Green came to see me and with one look at his tanned face I was instantly transported back to the Kirghizstan expedition, where we had been the previous summer.

There was a group of horsemen, fierce and with large moustaches. Each had a rifle slung over his shoulder. They decided to play a game involving a dead goat and ten or more furious equestrians. I was chosen to be 'it' and given the dead goat to look after whilst the rest of the tribesmen chased me through a dense apple orchard. When I say chosen, what I really mean to say is that I was the only volunteer. Johnny said he was far too whacked from the Khirgiz wrestling, Noel muttered something about being beaten at arm wrestling by a little lad (Noel stands six foot three and is twelve and a half stone), and Dave was nowhere to be seen, off reaping a certain five-leafed herbal remedy, no doubt. Up and down we galloped to the wide-eyed stares of my other team-mates, who didn't know I was this hot on a horse. I was keen to show off my equestrian skills and spun the horse around and around, until the whole world was a blur. Then I had the inevitable accident with a tree. A branch, too low, got in the way and swept me off my steed backward into the dirt. Apart from a few minor cuts and bruises I was unscathed and able to carry on with the expedition.

Stormont Murray was assigned to be my physiotherapist. He wasn't trained to be a neuro-physio but he knew a fair bit about the subject. Bespectacled, and black haired, he had the manner of a Clark Kent about him. He was also a keen climber and I think, when he could, he gave me much more than my allotted time in the gym. This was because I was a fellow climber but also because I was interested in my body and what he was doing with it. I was genuinely intrigued and asked why he requested me to slide curtain rails left and right or place cones on top of each other way over to my right. 'Standing balance,' he replied. I couldn't imagine people just doing what they're told, not questioning the basic principles of physiotherapy, not seeing that there was even a difference between neuro and orthopaedic physiotherapy. He was always keen to answer my questions. And he complained about how most people are overweight and it was hard to tell where a particular muscle was, the erecti spinae, for instance, or the obliques. I was like the illustrated man compared to these folk.

Barbara Hartfall was his senior and trained in neurophysiotherapy to boot. She only had three days with me and then was going on a month's holiday. She was not happy to be missing out on such an interesting case. In a provincial hospital it's not that often physios get special cases through their doors. OK, so I was just a stroke case to all intents and purposes, but I was a very severe stroke. I made good progress during my month in Ysbyty Gwynedd and Stormont said that I would be walking before the month was out. That meant the end of April. We would see.

My first day out amongst the hills was like the very first time. No. More intense. I didn't cry when I was younger and let loose in the hills. It was all so new and exciting, that was the last thought on my mind. I know a certain amount of my present emotion was my lability but it was still real as far as I was concerned. Celia and I lived in the heart of the Welsh hills so just going home to Llanberis took us right through them. We went the top way home, where I could see the summits and cwms, the green fields and pastures filled to brimming with cotton wool sheep and the blue grey of the quarry holes with their cone slag heaps, looking like a Wild West scene rather than Welsh countryside.

The purple ribbon of the Llanberis Pass road with Crib Goch and Crib y Ddysgl sitting like giant slate fans to the south with the Glyderau to the north; the interplay of light and darkness in just the right balance, switching and shifting like pieces in a game of chess, as the clouds move; the ruined farms, of which there are many, standing about like castles on their last legs; the strangely shaped plates of gravy down below at the bottom of the hillside that profess to be lakes – it was the minutiae that grabbed me and beckoned me to notice them. The two holly trees on the island in Llyn Glas that the sheep can't get to were planted by Celia's father who died a long time ago; the gate falling off its hinges; the boulder problem that I'd never seen before; the broken window in the school house at the top of Fachwen – it was as if I was trying to hold these minute things close to me and never ever let them go. Tears trickled down my cheeks from behind my cheap shades bought from Salamanca market.

At the farm, after Celia dragged me down the steps, I lay on the settee exhausted. We had an endless stream of visitors some of whom I hadn't seen since my accident. Sometimes I would have to send them all out of the room so that I could insert my catheter and relieve myself. Celia would cook me pasta pesto or carrot and coriander soup with a hunk of bread; it was a taste experience after the bland hospital food. Afterwards I would sit in the window and stare longingly at the mountains, wanting to turn the clock back, just a couple of months.

After two day visits home I was allowed out for the whole weekend. We put a bed downstairs, luckily we had a downstairs bathroom, and Celia could wheel me out into the garden to soak up the sunshine. From there I would while away the day attempting to read and appreciating the truly awesome view, punctuated with many naps on the bed. She said there wasn't enough space in the single bed for the two of us so she moved the futon downstairs to be near me. This touched me greatly. We would cuddle in the single bed and watch videos together or listen to music.

As my month in Ysbyty Gwynedd progressed I became more powerful in my left arm and leg while the recovery of my right side was frustratingly slow. I was so unsteady on my feet that if I ever stood up I could topple over at any moment, and frequently did so. After a couple of weeks spent self-catheterising I gradually wanted to piss more and more of my own volition. This was a dramatic turn of events and for a while I struggled, sometimes having to use the catheter and sometimes not. I had to learn to be patient, Gwyneth told me, and leave my bladder to fill at its normal pace. Every time I went to piss I would have to measure the residual in my bladder by shoving that tube up my cock again and presenting the cardboard bottle to the nurses to have it recorded on a chart. This made me feel like a child – 'Look, nurse, at what I've done' – and I hated the procedure. So I failed to do it almost every time, much to the dismay of Gwyneth who chided me with a musical Welsh accent. In the end she brought a machine with a LCD on it and, putting jelly on my abdomen, proceeded to carry out an ultrasound scan. Then she took the handful of tubes from me and said, 'You won't be needing those any more, Mr Pritchard.'

A wave of anxiety swept over me. 'What if I can't go?' Images of my bladder swelling up like a football and bursting in a shower of blood and urine filled my mind.

'Just relax, you'll know when it's time to go,' she replied in an exaggeratedly sympathetic manner.

I still could not read to the end of a line on a printed page. It was as if only the left-hand half of the page existed; I couldn't even see the right-hand half so didn't think to read it. This hemianopia is a classic symptom of hemiplegia but I only learnt this much later by reading up on it. My reading skills still had some way to go and I worried that it would always be thus. Someone brought in the *Weekend Guardian* interview I did for Sabine Durant and I was surprised to read the headline 'Rocks in the Head'. I hadn't seen it before and I wondered if she knew something that I didn't. I asked her not to dwell too heavily on my previous accidents but that was basically all it was about. People do have a morbid interest in accidents and I guess it's only natural that she should concentrate on them.

Ruth was the social worker assigned to me. This caring woman helped us fill in the scores of forms for the Severe Disablement Allowance and Disability Living Allowance amongst others. We couldn't have done it without her. I was struggling to write anything with my left hand and the forms were bewildering anyway. Whenever I attempted to write it was an illegible mess, as if a cockroach had dipped its feet into an inkpot and walked over the page. Ruth just whipped through them as only someone who is well practised at form-filling can. She was on the édge of retirement and soon to leave the area for a house that she and her husband had purchased on the Sound of Harris in the Outer Hebrides. Wearing short hair, cords and a checked shirt she looked as though she might have been a tomboy in her school days, if not still. She invited Celia and me to stay with her in the croft, which she'd had for years, waiting for this moment.

My good friend Sue Upton, who is a trained osteopath, came in twice a week at that time to give me cranial therapy. I'd had it before for all sorts of problems and found it very beneficial. Don't ask me to explain what it does, it's something about manipulating the cerebral spinal fluid. Anyway it makes you feel really weird for a while and, afterwards, much better. She said that my fluid was all pooling in the right side of my body and was basically all messed up. Pat Ingle also came to visit me; she's a masseuse. I can't begin to tell you how good it felt to have my leg and arm simply rubbed. They were still wooden but deep down they now had some feeling. I'm convinced that massage helps limbs regain lost feeling by sensitising them again.

A Dr Atara, my consultant, came in one morning and spoke to Celia as if I wasn't there. He was asking her questions about my condition while I was sitting right there in front of him. OK, so I must have sounded stupid because I stuttered somewhat but I felt I was totally coherent. Just because I'm in a wheelchair doesn't mean I'm not compos mentis and, even if I wasn't, he still could have made an effort to talk to me. Apart from Salamanca market where people behaved distinctly oddly with me, staring because I looked a right state, that was the first time I'd noticed the 'Does he take sugar' syndrome. Generally doctors know better and he was the last one to treat me in this way.

Tracey the occupational therapist came in that evening and made me transfer from my bed into a wheelchair that had weighing scales secreted under the seat. We had a laugh when I suggested that she was weighing me for my coffin. She scribbled down eleven stone in her notebook, put me back in my bed and pushed the weighing chair away.

Shortly afterwards a beautiful nurse of Indian origin, came to give me my medication. This included two paracetamol tablets, a Nizatadine tablet to stop any excess acid being produced and thereby creating an ulcer, and an anti-inflammatory suppository. She donned the rubber glove and ordered me to roll over. I was used to having things shoved up my bum by now and even looked forward to it in a perverse sort of way.

I now had a place at Clatterbridge on the Wirral Peninsula, Merseyside. At sixty miles distance it was the nearest neurological rehabilitation unit to North Wales. The leaving date was earmarked for the 5th April and it was the 2nd already. I had been lingering in Bangor for a whole month, which was OK from the point of view that I got to see all my friends from Wales but not so good from the rehab angle. It was all something to do with the financial year ending on the 1st April and Ysbyty Gwynedd not being able to afford to send me to the rehab unit until the new financial year came about. I think. But that was OK, I could live with that and besides Stormont and his colleague, Penny Croxford, who I was going to see a lot of more than half a year later, were absolutely ace physiotherapists.

I was supposed to travel by ambulance but Celia talked them into letting me ride in the car with her. The most enduring image I have, as we burned down the coast road, were those daffodils on the central reservation past Llanfairfechan. Their faces seemed sadder and more raggedy than a month earlier but thousands of them were still keeping their heads afloat in the good loam.

8

CLATTERBRIDGE DIARY

---

*People ask me what was it like, and I say yes, of course it
was dramatic and graphic and all that stuff, but at times it
was just kind of comic and strange. It was, I suppose, my
life-changing story.*

Ben Watt,
Patient

23rd April
Wirral Neurological Rehabilitation Unit, Clatterbridge

I don't know where to start this diary, so I'll start by describing
the inmates. They're a mixed bunch, from the victims of vicious
attacks with baseball bats to drink-drivers to victims of MS to a
whole host of mystery illnesses. The one binding factor is that
they all involve a neurological slant and the job of the staff here
is to integrate the patient back into society. This job may take one
month or it may take two years. Which one I would be I had no
idea. I must say that I've been here since the 4th April but only
now have I felt cognitively able to record my verbal diary into
my dictaphone. (And I didn't begin typing it up until mid-June.)

There's Gary who walks on tiptoes, due to a shortening of his
Achilles tendons. If you have spent a few months in a coma, like
him, and you're not using your feet, this is inevitable. He has
speech problems like I do. After a bottle and a half of vodka he
went driving in his new Audi, rolling down an embankment and
giving himself a brain injury. He's got a tribe of misbehaving kids

91

and a wife, he says, who is cheating on him. They are forever arguing. It hardly seems like the ideal environment for recovery. I grimace when his tribe comes in. They are ugly and cheeky brats who race up the corridor and around the day room.

He hasn't learnt any manners off his folks and he sure as hell isn't passing any on to his kids. He plays Hardcore, a type of techno-music with people shouting, at high decibels all day long, not giving a toss that I'm trying to work. He passes his photos of the wrecked car proudly round to all my mates. Stunned, they laugh nervously.

There's Smithy, a big-time drug-dealer who was being driven by a twenty-one-year-old girl who died as a result of a collision with a lamp post which then fell on top of them. He is bald on top, wears a beard and has no teeth bar a couple at the sides. He jokes that he left them on the dashboard of the car. Smithy's always one for chatting up the nurses and having rum and Coke brought in for him by 'the missus'.

He has hideous nightmares stemming from the accident which he can only steer away from by using a cocktail of drugs, twenty milligrams of Diazepam, Tylex and a couple of cans of Special Brew. They tried to cut him down to ten milligrams but, as he says, 'I can get as many Diazies as I want for fifty pee a piece off the bag-heads by us.'

He's got a 'dense hemi' of the right side as well, so it is pretty interesting comparing notes. But if one thing has become apparent it is that no two head injuries are the same, even if they have similar symptoms. Such things as length of time before emergency treatment (Smithy was only forty minutes, as opposed to my ten hours) and the severity of the injury are all-important factors. Smithy is well on the road to recovery now, while I am still in this wheelchair and our injuries were about the same time. It starts you thinking, what have I done to deserve this? But that would be wishing harm on yourself. You have to have faith in the brain's power to heal itself, you have to keep saying, yes I can get through this, and keep thinking positive.

There's Kevin, a seventeen-year-old lad whose friend was driving when he had his accident. As far as I can get the story straight the driver's sister was killed in the accident and he put Kevin in this sorry state. The driver was drunk and is now serving a two-year sentence. Doubly incontinent, Kevin can't walk without a rollater and shouts obscenities at any one who cares to listen, except his parents. He is what psychologists call 'disinhibited' which means that he'll swear like blue murder. Not all the time, some times he wouldn't say boo to a goose, but at others, especially when he's doing physiotherapy, he'll kick off. 'Get off my cock, you fucking cunt,' he will say to the nurses when they try to change his Convene, a condom which you piss into; or 'I'm not doing it, you hairy-arsed whore', to Sian Hughes the physiotherapist.

Then there's Bri, again a drug-dealer, but small-time compared to Smithy. He woke up one morning and found he had a virus on his spine. He's now in a motorised wheelchair at twenty-eight. He's got a skinhead and listens to Metallica and Slayer all day long. He is basically completely paralysed, apart from his left hand with which he controls a joystick to steer himself.

He seems to be having a relationship with Alison who is seventeen years old, and you wouldn't think a day older. She has milk bottle white skin and wiped her memory out in a car crash. She went driving with her then boyfriend and took a dive through the windscreen of a BMW borrowed from the lad's father. He was seventeen also. He never came in to see her once and she hates him and drenches him in scorn. When she first came in here she had to be taken to the toilet because she had forgotten where it was and, later, she would misplace all the nurses' names, even though she had been here months. It's sweet to see young love. Everywhere that Bri motored Alison would follow. She is totally physically able and just looks at odds following one step behind a guy in a motorised wheelchair.

Sheila who walks but only just is a pretty, proud woman who used to be in high-flying business until this dreadful affliction hit her. All the skin started to peel off her body, starting at her inner thigh and, when I came in, she was skinless. It looked like she had a very good suntan, until upon closer inspection that is, and she had to wear a wig. She stayed in her room, watching daytime TV, most of the time. Then, like a shy animal, she started being tempted out of her den, to the vast empty spaces of the day room. It would be easy for us, the other inmates, to say, 'Don't worry about how you look, we're all in the same kettle to a greater or lesser degree.' But that would be to deny her sensibilities.

We have Tom who came off a motorcycle, (although he'd have you know it was a car crash,) in the Caribbean and hit a bollard. He's very slow and muddles his words and is always complaining to the doctors about when he will be let out of here. It's as if he doesn't realise his own problem. 'He's an architect, for God's sake. How will he get it together to do technical drawings and behave in a professional manner towards clients?' I heard Ms Caroline Young, the consultant neurologist for the ward, mention quietly in the corridor. Tom has a wife who is still out working in Jamaica and comes to visit him once every couple of months. It must be really sad and frustrating for him, being away from his home and wife.

There's also an old lady called Jean who is always trying to escape, which keeps the staff on their toes. She hasn't got any teeth and loves to do jigsaw puzzles. Her only visitor is her husband who looks Tibetan and smells of Woodbines. Jean is very disoriented and asks if anybody has seen the wooden horse, the coalbunker, or the Christmas decorations. One day she escaped out of the kitchen door, walked all the way around the building, and entered the Oncology Department before the nurses could scramble and go and find her.

4th May

I feel very resentful of able-bodied people who can just get up and walk or go where they want to. People who can still go rock climbing and surfing and sailing or simply just walking around and feeling the fresh air. I don't know if I'll ever be able to do these things again. Of course I put a brave face on the situation and tell everybody that I'm doing fine but deep down I'm obviously not doing fine by anyone's stretch of the imagination.

I had an idea to photograph all the inmates, just take portraits of them all, but I don't know how they'll react to that. Apparently I need special permission off all the relatives involved, so I knocked that one on the head. We watched a sad movie called *Awakenings* the other night and I mean really sad. All I could do was laugh all the way through it and that upset Celia no end. She couldn't get to grips with the fact that I really wanted to cry but it came out in hysterics. Thank goodness it was on video and not at the cinema.

When I first came here I could stand, but that was it. I definitely couldn't walk and in the past four weeks I've come on a hell of a lot thanks to Sian and Nina, her helper. Sian has to put up with my giggling fits, at least it's more of a laugh than crying all the time, like I was before. I seemed to switch from crying to laughing overnight. It could be her infectious good humour that has had a healing effect. I never laugh with such vigour with any of my other therapists. I spat in Sian's eye today I was laughing so much and Nina had to fetch me a tissue to wipe it out with. This is still part of my lability and at times my laughter is inappropriate and it worries me a little. I was in hysterics when I heard the news about Linda McCartney's death on the television and Ella, an old patient with MS, who was trying to watch, said that it was disgraceful that I should laugh at a time like this. It's just when I'm nervous that it grabs me. There was one time when a friend of mine told me of her father who had a disease which made him fall over all the time. This was a really bad time to giggle or even grin but I did and went crimson with embarrassment.

Sian has the blonde side of red hair and her yellow belt at karate. She asks me things like, 'Is there anything functional you could do with your right hand previously that you can't do now?' It only took one glance at her for me to burst into laughter. She's going soon as part of her four monthly rotations. I'm going to miss her and her look of incredulity every time I crack up.

I took my first few steps last week. Though they were undoubtedly Frankenstein's monster steps, they were steps nevertheless. That's three months after my accident. Alas, they put me back into a wheelchair because the pattern of walking was all wrong. If you start walking too early, as can be seen with patients who had their injury in the 'sixties, you could have a marked limp for the rest of your life. So it's back to the chair for me until I develop a style of walking that is usable.

My hip control is improving with every day that passes and the abductor muscles seem to be kicking in. I can tell that because my knee doesn't flop in as badly when I stand up. They're all good signs.

7th May

Fiona Parry, my neuro-psychologist, put me through a series of gruelling cognitive tests and intelligence tests for two whole weeks. Every day for one hour. Puzzles and mental arithmetic, recognising obscure shapes and doing word tests. Essentially IQ tests. She estimated that I was above average intelligence pre-morbid, before my accident, and well below average (an IQ of 90), post-morbid. She had some problems estimating this, as I have virtually no academic qualifications, so she just went on my previous book and a handful of O-levels. I described how I was having memory problems and concentration difficulties. I found learning new names particularly hard and I lost track whilst reading several times per page. My performance on PASAT, a test of sustained attention thought to be a sensitive indicator of the ability to return to work, was significantly impaired.

Yesterday we had patients singing along to Elvis Presley on the tape machine. It's astounding how many Elvis impersonators there are. I laughed till my stomach ached seeing Alison and Kevin straining to find the chords of 'In the Ghetto'. Kevin was dead flat in a voice way too low for his seventeen years and Alison caterwauled at a piercing pitch.

There's a new patient here called Dave who's suffering from MS. He's hilarious and takes the piss out of every one mercilessly with his Marty Feldman eyes. He's had MS for twenty-five years and has been in a wheelchair for ten. His legs and feet are frozen out straight in a grotesque caricature of a ballet dancer in the *pas de deux*. He is waiting to have his ankles and knees snapped. But that won't be for a few years he says. Such is the NHS.

When he was in his twenties he worked the oceans as a merchant seaman. He has been everywhere, from Bombay to Buenos Aires, from Nairobi to New York. Then one night in mid-Atlantic, as he was changing watch, he went to descend a ladder and fell the full length of it. The captain, thinking he was drunk, put him in a locked cabin until the end of the voyage. When he still behaved like a drunk after a week in solitary the captain knew he had made a mistake. 'They put me in hospital,' he complained, 'but they couldn't find anything wrong with me. That's the strange thing about this disease, it's fuckin' hard to diagnose, and when they did find out, I was the last one to know about it. They kept it from me for ten fuckin' years.'

It shows true strength that he has kept his astonishing brand of humour in the face of overwhelming adversity. For the last ten years he has been in a first-floor flat day and night. People visit him when they choose to, though he doesn't have many friends and he certainly doesn't go out visiting. The ambulance women have to carry him downstairs in a stretcher.

'When you look like this people think it's OK to stare. They think you're stupid as well as deformed.' He breaks into a mock expression of an archetypal 'spastic'. 'So I'm not bothered about living on the first floor, who gives a flying fuck about goin' out anyway.'

Last night Jean got into bed with Smithy. He was asleep and thought that he was getting a visitation from his wife. When he put his arm around her to give her a cuddle something mustn't have seemed quite right and he woke up with a scream.

'What the fuck!'

She calmly said, 'Shut up and budge up.'

The night nurses all came running when they heard the commotion and began bellowing with laughter. Gary and I slept through it. Smithy never tires of telling that story and each time it gets more outrageous. He blames Gary and me for not waking up.

I was looking on the timetable for weeks before I realised what S.a.L.T. meant. It wasn't until my first appointment with Siobhan, my speech and language therapist, that I got it. She was a bubbly woman who I couldn't stop grinning at. They're used to that though. Inane grinning is the least of their worries. They have to put up with verbal abuse regularly and sometimes physical assault. Siobhan said that I was well on my way to mental recovery and this was evidenced by the fact that I was contemplating writing my second book.

18th May

I had my leg cast this morning which is an attempt to stop me going onto tiptoes every time I straighten my leg – an associated reaction.

It's been boiling hot now for ten days and I'm getting a tan. All the nurses, physios, OTs and orderlies are out sunning themselves and eating their lunch at the picnic tables in the courtyard. It's a real garden party atmosphere, especially with music playing. It makes a real difference having the quadrant to sit in, even if it is caged off from the outside world. I couldn't imagine not having greenery about me. I'm sure it's one of the things that keeps me sane, along with writing this diary.

I named nineteen animals in a minute the other day, compared to three in Bangor. So that says something for my mental processing speed. About twenty is the average, but I've been practising my animals, so I fear I wouldn't fare so well on the names of, say, fruits or foods.

The Wisconsin Card Sort, which I did with Fiona a few weeks ago, was kind of interesting. It goes like this: you have at least a hundred cards in a pack, which is divided into any number up to four, of squares, triangles, circles and stars. These are all different colours, too. Four cards are put in front of you. The rules are that you must match cards up by your own rules. At first it was easy, matching by shape, stars to stars, circles to circles, that kind of thing. Then she tells you that the rules have changed and again it's obvious what you should do. Match by number, four triangles to four squares, three circles to three stars. Then she tells you that the rules have changed yet again and that you have to guess how. It may seem obvious to you that they be matched by colour, but I couldn't grasp this. We turned and turned, me thinking up ever more unlikely combinations, until all the cards were gone.

It never occurred to me until Celia said, 'What about colour?' as if it were obvious. Being colour blind, I have never trusted colour as a way of categorising objects. I never see the colour of a person's eyes, even after I've known them for ten years. So even though those cards were the most familiar gaudy colours, I still didn't think to categorise by them. That's my theory anyway.

The occupational therapist specialises in one's functional ability and Lise Satherley had me doing similar tests but perhaps slightly easier. I had to build a coat hanger out of wire with written instructions and then build a tower following photographic instructions. It was elementary stuff, if you weren't brain damaged; I made some mistakes following the written instructions and trying to use the jig that was presented to me.

I had no trouble at all following pictorial instructions, though they were quite complicated. That's maybe because I spent a vast portion of my life following topo diagrams for climbs. So that may go part way to explaining why I've always been useless at following cookery recipes and yet have no problem with the visual side of things. My climber's mind has always solved problems by vision.

I had a good memory for diagrams but not for stories, I had a good memory for pictures but not for writing. That has made writing this book doubly difficult. As soon as I get an idea for a sentence in the day room I have to come rushing back to my ward, in my wheelchair, only to find that the idea has completely evaporated.

'Who is the President of the United States? Who is the Prime Minister of the United Kingdom? What year are we in? What month is it? What date is it? What day of the week is it? What time do you think it is?' These are questions that Fiona and Lise ask me all the time, as if it is *prima facie* evidence I am demented if I don't know the answers. But I never know what day of the week it is anyway, and I've never had a watch to tell the time by in my life. These aren't things you need to know when you are a climber. You get up when the day dawns, regardless of which day of the week it is, and you go climbing. I have been known not to know which year we're in even before my accident.

An ECG was put on me this morning, ten shiny metallic stickers all linked up to a pencil that sketches the electric patterns of your heart. I had been taking Phenytoin ever since that rock hit me, to save me from convulsing, and in my last blood sample I had dangerously high levels of the drug. I had been complaining of feeling unusually drowsy and after my ECG the doctors cut my amount drastically, with a view to stopping it all together.

The pills were replaced straight away by an injection into my belly, a blood anti-coagulant, which I have to administer myself every morning. I have to wear sexy thigh-length stockings as well, again to prevent blood clots, veins thrombosing.

19th May

I can feel a nervous energy reaching my legs and feet, my arms and fingers. A nearly but not quite feeling.

It's funny how not only can I not move my limbs but also I have forgotten how to move them. I have forgotten the very concept of movement. My lefts limbs are working just as they should but on my right side things are far from normal. Spasticity tends to override every movement. When I walk just a few steps my arm comes up as if it's got a life of its own. And my leg tends to fix into a pattern of extension, standing me on tiptoe, the whole limb rigid.

Then, all of a sudden, my brain remembers how to use the pectorals, say, as if it had been using them all along, or had never forgotten in the first place. Then I'll forget again and it's lost. Occasionally I'll remember but not quite enough, so that I am tingling all over my foot and hand, all over my arm and leg, but still no movement. Like an electrical current when the fuse is blown, it reaches the plug but not the appliance.

Today in physio I was working on isolating the quadracep, the thigh, and tensing it. Previously my thigh and glute would just wobble like jelly, but in the last couple of weeks they've settled down, unless I've really pushed them – by that I mean ten minutes standing instead of five. I'm overworking the muscles that I do have on my right side to compensate for those which I don't have. These muscles then require constant massaging and loosening up to dampen the effect down.

When I first came to this place I felt like I'd walked straight into *One Flew Over the Cuckoo's Nest*. There was all the moanings of the Chronics, and all the droolings of the Disturbeds and plenty of Big Nurses. There was even a Bull Goose Loony. But now that I've been here a couple of months I've started calling it home. 'Take me home,' I'll say without thinking to whoever is to bring me back that weekend. It's as far as one can get from *One Flew*

Over the Cuckoo's Nest – the staff are all, without exception, selfless and kind.

What's called 'associated reactions' are something many people find surprising. When I yawn my arm rears up and my leg shoots out. People expect paralysed to mean just that, dormant, without any movement. That was the case for the first month but then weird things started to happen. If I'm not careful these could develop into severe spasticity. In my case it's a pattern of flexion in the arm and extension in the leg. At first I encouraged this because it was the only sign of movement in my crippled body. The only evidence of tone in the otherwise flaccid half of my person. But then I began to notice a tightening of the bicep and hamstring so I could no longer straighten my arm or leg.

I then began noticing, when I lay flat on my back, supine, my toes turn upwards, my foot points downwards and my whole leg tenses. It feels great to stretch out, but I have no control over it. Whenever I lie down it simply happens. I only have flexion tendons at the moment, flexion muscles. I have no extensors. This is most evident in my arm where, if I'm not careful to stretch it out, my wrist and elbow can curl up skywards, clawing up like the typical spastic pattern.

Again I encouraged the associated reaction in my leg so much so that the physio had to cast it. Sitting here with that cast on I realise my mistake. It creates a pattern, which is reinforced in your reptilian brain or brain stem, so that every time you yawn that's what will happen. The reptilian brain is, as the name implies, the most distant, evolutionarily speaking and deals with sweating, goose bumps and impulse reactions such as pulling your hand out of a fire. It's what we learn to toddle on and what creates these associated reactions.

A recurring dream grabs me and won't let me go. It is of running across fields, free, free from this nightmare that is still there when I wake in the morning. Free to take flight across meadows of long summer grass. Running, sprinting for all my life's worth. And that's it, just running. The wheelchair standing by my bed gives the game away. Sometimes I think that I'm normal and healthy until I turn over and see *it* there. That cursed thing that I can't live without.

22nd May

A big day. The woman I love decided it would be best if we didn't see each other again on a romantic level. In other words she has left me. She broke the news in the van whilst bringing me back from hospital. She parked up in a lay-by because she couldn't see through the tears.

All I could do was break down into laughter. I laughed until I couldn't laugh any more. The laughter then turned to tears. Tears of sadness. There were a lot of good memories tied up in those six years of togetherness. And the fact that she saved my life must surely mean that I am eternally indebted to her.

Sitting on top of Shiprock in the four corners of the USA, on the summit of El Aleta de Tiburon (The Shark's Fin), in the Towers of Paine, Chile, swimming in the middle of the night on a midsummer Isle of Eigg, watching the sun rise up from the forests of Borneo on Kinabalu, alone, together, setting up the camera and taking your picture on the shoulder of Trango Tower in Pakistan, skinny dipping in Lago Nordenskold, Chile and you proposing we get it together by the bridge across the Ganga in Uttarkashi, India. All these memories make me warm inside my belly to remember.

But all I can think about now is the weight that has been lifted from me, as if I was being trapped in a gloved fist, and suddenly set free. All I have to look after now is myself. I don't have to think about anybody else. I can concentrate on the mammoth task of getting myself better. My rehabilitation has to come first. Sad as it may be, that's the way it is. There seems something oddly amusing about a life in ruins. Not only am I a raspberry ripple, a hemiplegic, but my girlfriend has left me as well. That's what it

103

seems like at first. When I told her that I loved her on the telephone there was only a terrifying silence for a response. It was like I was talking into a void, a black echoing box, where my own words were cast back at me.

'A psychic kick up the backside,' that's what Sue Duff in Tasmania had said. And she was right. I would still be carrying on the same life as before if it were not for this accident. Instead I was embarking on a whole new adventure, where nothing was certain. Just how I like it and will grow to accept it.

Celia took me down to Walton Hospital for an appointment with Mr Foy this morning. The first thing he did was to take a tape measure out of his pants pocket and assess the length and width of the wound.

'It's a jolly sizeable gash you've got on your head there,' he declared. 'About five inches by, let's see, two and a half. Now, Mr Pritchard, having seen your scans, there seems to be a very big shadow which would suggest to me that you have sustained a large amount of damage.' I thought, tell me something I don't know. He then 'suggested' to me in the same polite manner 'that your climbing days are almost certainly over'. I replied somewhat indignantly, 'We'll see about that.' What right has he to play God like that when he doesn't even know me? It is the first time he has ever met me. How can he say such a thing, when he doesn't know the will power I possess?

Anyway he also said that I wouldn't have my head plated for at least three years, if ever. Something about the risk of further trauma to the brain being too great. Apparently my scalp has healed directly onto my brain and a very precise surgical operation would have to be carried out to pare the two apart. It suits me if I never have it done. At least I will get to keep my party trick. I have discovered that if I hold my nose, and create pressure in my head, I can make my brain swell so that my scalp rises by about an inch. I call it flipping my wig.

At the end of March I wiggled my toes but only three times and then it disappeared, I couldn't wiggle them any more. I suppose

I'm scared breaking up with Celia will put my rehab back. I have to keep thinking positive which is really difficult at a time like this. The physios always stress the importance of positive thinking and that the right mental attitude will win through. I feel as though I'm cracking like a pigeon's fragile eggshell.

25th May

Fiona, the neuro-psychologist counselled me, and I told my story about our relationship break-up from start to finish. She said that numerous relationships break up after head injuries. Lack of sexual function that sometimes arises from a crack on the head is often responsible. Or the change in roles can be the cause, the breadwinner suddenly unable to work. It was neither of those things for us, we just drifted apart. The accident wasn't the cause of the break-up; rather the break-up was a symptom of the accident.

I went house-hunting today but it's a difficult task as many of the houses have steps up to them or only upstairs toilets. There are no bungalow in Llanberis but I couldn't live anywhere else. The true extent of non-wheelchair friendliness in towns and cities hits you like a lead banana when you're in one.

1st June

Andrew is a new admission who has a severe head injury and keeps repeating himself again and again. He is bearded, ginger-haired, balding. He doesn't smile and complains about the food all the time. From down the corridor he sounds like a horse race commentator when he's being disinhibited. Even Bazza, who helps with the serving of meals and is usually so pleasant with patients, comes back despairing when he has been to serve Andrew his dinner. His wife says that he has always been grumpy and that it isn't a result of the car accident. He even has a sign on his door saying 'KNOCK BEFORE ENTERING' – in a hospital!

The whole right side of my body went into spasm today. I was lying on my bed when I sensed what I can only describe as an intense déjà vu, more intense than any I had felt before. I had definitely been in this situation before and I knew what was going to happen next. A rhythmic twitching in my toes soon began. I got off the bed because I knew Tricia Rodgers, my senior physiotherapist, and Lise were on the patio and I was keen to show them this latest phenomenon. I manoeuvred myself into my chair and wheeled out to them.

By the time I'd reached them I was experiencing something I hadn't felt before. It was a throbbing pulse, waves of tingling travelling up my right leg from my foot to my fingertips. My leg was still in a cast and when Trish tried to bend my toes up I screamed out in pain. It was like boiling water being poured into my pot.

She then attempted to straighten my leg but it was locked in a right angle, such was the flexion exerted by my hamstring. Then my arm began to feel detached. It floated out to the side; it wasn't mine any more. That was a feeling I haven't had for some time now, maybe three months. They wheeled me up the ramp, through the French windows and put me to bed. After an hour in bed I was on top of the world again.

Ever since the spasm it's like something's about to happen, some movement's about to start. Later that afternoon, about two hours after, I moved my ankle and then my knee. That was a massive step forward; not only did I have my upper leg but my lower leg is coming in now as well. I only moved them a fraction of an inch but that is a start. Things can only improve and get stronger.

It turns out that what I experienced was a seizure, an abnormal electrical discharge in my brain. A 'simple partial seizure' only affects the opposite side of the body to the damaged hemisphere of the brain. This was a 'late seizure', which is generally associated with more severe brain injuries, involving damage to the brain surface. From what I can gather there were fragments of skull pushed onto the brain and blood leaked into the area, bathing the surface of the organ. This haemorrhage was especially irritating and likely to cause a seizure disorder. It produces what is known as the Jacksonian March. The attack begins with jerks of a single part of the body, such as a finger, and then spreads to other fingers and so to the whole hand and then the arm. This guy called Jackson noticed, in 1870, that wherever the lesion was in the cortex of the brain, the corresponding part of the body would fit.

So it's back on the Phenytoin for me which is less than ideal. It strips me mentally of all my creativity, makes me severely drowsy, robs me of life. The déjà vu bit is a common symptom of having fits. It's called the 'aura'.

We were watching a TV documentary this evening and it showed a ferret with cataracts. In a rehabilitation unit for brain-injured patients we were watching a programme about a ferret with cataracts! We simultaneously burst into laughter, Smithy spraying us with tea and toast as he has a habit of doing.

2nd June

I can't sleep because I'm brimming over with excitement. My whole right side feels like it's coming to life, tingling, and pins and needles. I'm wide-awake, perhaps it's the drugs making me more alert. I want to write everything down.

I have to inject myself every morning directly into my belly. This is to administer a blood anti-coagulant. It was rather unpleasant at first, needling myself in the stomach, but it got easier. The staff of this place have decided to let me administer all my own medication now. This self-regulation is supposed to give me that extra degree of independence and make me feel like I'm looking out for myself, making my own decisions. I don't think they realise just how independent I am but I'll humour them.

3rd June

I took a fall in the toilet when I twisted over on my ankle. It was a desperate struggle to get myself back up once I was down and, though the nurses' alarm cord was right in front of me, I was determined to get up without assistance. Perhaps I was also a little embarrassed to be down on the bog floor. There's a stainless steel guardrail, which is meant to stop you from falling. I somehow avoided it and landed, in my underpants, on the wet tiles. It was the rail that I climbed, hand over greasy hand; back up with my legs hugging the bowl like it was a tree that I was trying to save. When I eventually got to my feet, I needed a shower to wash off all that stale piss and God knows what else lurking around the base of a toilet bowl.

The dynamics of the fish tank are very interesting. It reminds me of going snorkelling with Celia round the coral reefs of Mamutik and Sapi. I spend hours a day watching the bullies and weaklings. There isn't any rhyme or reason to who's top fish. Sometimes it's a big angelfish bullying a little platty but just as often the king of the tank will be a little tiger barb. The gourami will often be the one to throw its weight around. They're silver with long trailers coming from their mouths. Apparently, so Fish Man says, they live in muddy water and survive in conditions that would kill all the other fish. The plec had nothing to do with such insignificance until they killed and ate it. You need a plecostamus to keep the glass clean because they hoover up all the algae that sticks to it. Fish Man, who comes in once a month to tend to the tank, brought a new monster specimen in this week, presumably one that could hold its own with the other fish. He had been growing it for three years and no sooner had he put it in the water, it turned from a black colour to a pale grey and looked rather ill. But the other fish don't want to mess with it because it's a big brute of a thing.

6th June

I'm now within the average range for verbal fluency. This is where you have to think of as many words as possible beginning with a certain letter in one minute. I thought of nineteen words beginning with the letter C: Chicken, chip, chat, chubby . . . that sort of thing. That's a dramatic increase, considering that while I was at Ysbyty Gwynedd I could only think of three words beginning with T and they were tea, tee and think!

I couldn't move my foot today, whereas yesterday I could, so that was a little disappointing. My knee would only move by invoking a serious reaction in my right hand but at least it would move. I should know better than to get all depressed but any time that I get a muscle working and then it stops again, as so often happens, I get downhearted.

Some people still don't know how to take me. They can clam up as one friend did when he came to collect me and drive me home from the Unit. He wouldn't look me in the eye and didn't know what to say, even though he was usually so talkative. 'I won't bite. You can look at me you know,' I said cruelly. He muttered some apologies and proceeded to meet my gaze more.

Those that don't know me see the chair first and foremost and they see me as an extension of the chair. They don't know how to relate to me and act kind of nervous. My friends see me first and they don't even notice the chair. So with a stranger it's hard to avoid talking about your disability and how it affects you. 'How did you get to be in a wheelchair?' they will ask. And usually I will answer just to avoid appearing rude. With my friends, well, they're already bored with hearing it and would prefer to talk about something else.

What is much more frustrating are those who pretend I'm not there. It doesn't happen often, but when it does I hate this chair and myself. Admittedly it's not my close friends that do this. It's more my acquaintances, those who I just know to say 'hi' to.

They look at you yet through you, they look into your eye but then find something much more interesting on your left shoulder. Then they turn away as if they never saw a thing. What kind of culture is it that breeds these cripple-o-phobes?

Alison had her accident on the same day as I, Friday the 13th February. Knowing this brought us closer together for a few moments, as if the common bond of a shared accident date actually meant something. But alas, no sooner had it become a fact, something tangible, than it was gone, a flight of fancy, along with each of the nurse's names and her memory of just about everything else.

When Celia and I split we hadn't been sharing a bed for perhaps four months because I was in various hospitals and institutions. So continuing in that way was by far the easier part. It was her support that I missed. I once said that she was my lover, my mother and my sister all rolled into one. It seemed as though I were devoid of anyone to talk to, to cry with, to laugh with, for there often are hilarious moments in these situations, to share my experience with. But my friends are being astounding, really rallying round. Not once have I got the ambulance to or from Clatterbridge because there is always Noel Craine or Adam Wainwright or Charlie Diamond, and many more there to take me.

I've been told that I haven't to walk. Tricia said that if I do it would create a wrong pattern of movement which, if I'm not careful, will persist and keep on persisting. 'So you have to be patient as well as determined.'

She thought intensely for a moment. 'A conflict of interest immediately presents itself. How is it possible to be patient and determined at the same time?'

I sat on the bench, just wearing shorts after one of our physio sessions and quietly asked, How?

'Find the determination and anything is possible.'

I replied irritably, 'But it's counter-intuitive to sit in a chair when you know you can walk, of sorts. If I had a serious leg injury you would get me standing on it as soon as you thought safe. But I guess it's different with a brain injury. Are you going to keep me in the chair until you think I have a normal pattern of walking, which could be years from now?'

'You cannot bend your knee, you see.' I took a step and immediately saw. 'So you are hitching up at your hip. This is a bad pattern of movement and you do not want the leg to stay like that for the rest of your life. Do you?' I agreed I did not. 'The injured brain recognises the motor patterns that are most familiar and routes them from another place in the brain. There is a term for it, neuro-plasticity. The brain is a much more plastic organ than we previously thought. It is capable of adapting and learning as your environment changes.'

'So you're telling me that parts of the brain can learn how to do the job of the previous and now injured part.'

'That's exactly what I'm saying.'

15th June

Alison says I look twenty-one. She is seventeen and has a traumatic brain injury, so I don't think I can trust her judgement. But lots of people say how well I'm looking. Either they were expecting me to look horrific and were surprised to see that I wasn't or the stone in weight I've put on suits me. Thing is, I feel completely healthy, the healthiest I've felt in years. My injury was five months ago and, apart from being in this chair, I feel fierce. Ready to face the outside world square on.

When I asked Fiona Parry, my neuro-psychologist, whether it was worth putting off my grief about the disintegration of my relationship until I had healed, she said it was good to talk out my problems. But I have decided that I shouldn't let a bit of negativity enter my head. I've just got to keep thinking positive if I'm going to get through this. That's difficult when you've had a bad accident and you're in a wheelchair and you've split up with your girlfriend and everything is going pear-shaped. But it is possible.

But I will get through this. I may not be climbing again but I have a philosophical approach and know that I've had just about all the experiences that a climber could wish for. On mile high walls I have been, dangling my feet over the edge of a portaledge, shouting 'You can't reach me up here!' Feeling the adrenaline pumping on high dizzy sea cliffs. Walking in up vast deserted glaciers in the Arctic. On *the* perfect boulder, when the friction is just right, and I've pulled the move off and done the problem I've been trying for ages. Or watching the sun go down in the Welsh hills, my favourite place, turning all red under a cloudscape the likes of which you've never seen.

I'll always need a climbing replacement, something that gives me that norepinephrine buzz. Writing can replace that, and it helps to keep me sane here in rehab, helps me make what sense there is of it all. But I'll need action, as well, if I'm to get that adrenaline fix. I'm talking flying or diving or snowy mountaineering.

My scapula started moving this week. Jill Chappel, my other physiotherapist, lifted my shoulder blade and, digging under it with her fingers, helped it along with lots of massage. Jill is my senior therapist at the minute. She has short black hair and cold hands, a soft Yorkshire accent, being from Ilkley, and dark eyes. When I came back today, Jill said I was walking better than ever, probably due to my hamstrings beginning to kick in for the first time in five months. OK, so that's only postural, but I'm sure it helps with my walking also.

I also removed the hemi-cuff because there was increased tone in my deltoid. I had been wearing this or other slings to stop my shoulder dislocating ever since week one. The shoulder joint is the weakest joint in the body. A soft tissue joint, it is held together only by tendons and ligaments and a capsule of sinovial fluid. The hemi-cuff is a type of sling forming a tube for the upper arm to go inside. It is then passed under the pit of the opposite arm, the tape forming a cross pattern on your back. I was the only person that the therapists knew of who could put one on myself using a

Fastex buckle thrown from behind over the shoulder. The joint feels very vulnerable now though, like it's swinging around on a flimsy bunch of ligaments, which is exactly what it is doing.

There's always something fresh about the start of the week. Everybody asks, 'How was your weekend?' and patients roll in throughout the day. There are the ambulance workers, one driver and one aid, who wheel James in, even though he can walk with a rollater. They wear white shirts and grey trousers. Sometimes there are new patients and you have to treat them warily in case they fly off the handle with you. And then, of course, there's the MS folks in for respite care while their families take a break in Benidorm or Majorca.

This diary is transcribed from a Dictaphone which I always keep with me. The times when I've forgotten to take it to the day room or, more serious, home at weekends, I don't have much time before I have a complete memory departure. I can hold a fact in my head for perhaps a minute before I lose it utterly. If it comes back to me the feeling is as though from a past life, so my life right now is a constant string of déjà vus. But this is improving at a slow rate.

Meals always consist of something in a milky sloppy cheesy sauce if you are vegetarian. Milky slop and two tasteless overboiled veg. Tapioca or rice pudding, more milky slop, follows this again. This is bad news if you are allergic to dairy products as I tend to be. But if we are lucky we get cheese and biscuits or sponge and custard.

My favourite part of the day is physiotherapy. Where else to you get stripped to your underpants and massaged by two beautiful women? I would say that a high percentage of the guys on the unit have a thing about the therapists. I guess it's classic to fall in love with your physio, especially if they're all as wonderful and caring as our therapists are. Jill and Tricia, at the moment, have me weight-bearing through my arm, though they have to be very careful not to damage my shoulder. They also have me walking up and down the physio gym but I'm having trouble with my knee hyper-extending. The gym is about sixteen feet in length and I can walk it four times. However, this damn knee keeps flicking back painfully.

15th June

The domestics, or stewardesses as they are now known, wearing pink dresses, are busying themselves around the ward this morning, sweeping, mopping and polishing the floor with something that looks like a vacuum cleaner. They come while we're still sleeping and give us fresh water jugs and when we wake up they bring us tea in bed. They serve us kak for dinner and kak for tea. But that's not their fault. It's the thin guy with the moustache sporting a heavily starched blue cotton suit pushing the insulated box. I've come to hate that moment when he pushes the blue box in through the sliding door.

17th June

The World Cup's been on for a week and each night we've crowded round the box watching it. Cheering on 'our boys'. Except those guys who've got money on some other country like the Netherlands or Argentina in the prize draw the Unit has set up.

I'm going through buying a house at the moment and there's talk of a council grant to put in a lift. If that happens I will own the only house in Llanberis with a lift shaft, a great big Tardis in the corner of the room. I could open it to the public. 'Roll up, roll up, come and ride the incredible, ascending lift.' Even though I can walk up stairs perfectly easily (kind of) the OTs, social worker and local council still have to play it safe and look on the most pessimistic side.

At first, when I'd just had my accident, I felt uneasy around

The Totem Pole.

(Left) 'It seemed rather strange to be on the summit first and then to descend from it only to climb up to it again.'

(Below) 'Suddenly I was two hundred feet above a thrashing swell not knowing to what the other end of the rope was attached.'

Some of the Tasmanian nursing team and therapists.
Back row, l-r: Kylie Burns, James Lloyd, Ian Watson,
Wendy Burton; *middle row, l-r:* Melissa Brodribb,
Moy Moy Pierce, Alanna McKay, Jenny Healy;
bottom row, l-r: Kris Clauson, Jane Boucher and Me.

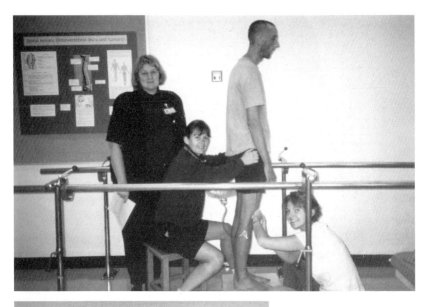

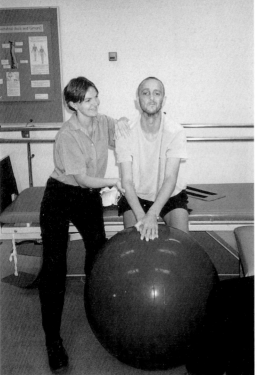

(Above) Physiotherapy with Dawn Lewis and Nicola Mackinnon. My speech therapist Marge Conroy standing by.

(Left) 'That smile seemed a grotesque caricature of my smile.' In the gym with physiotherapist Nicola Mackinnon.

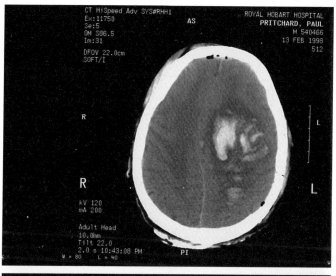

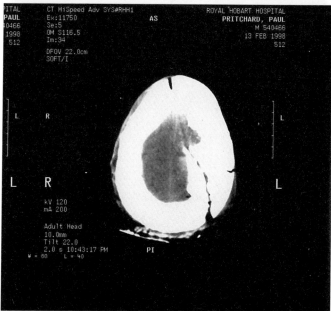

'The CT scans of my head from Tasmania looked shocking. There was a fuzzy white patch virtually covering the whole of the left hemisphere of my brain. The top scan shows the midline shift of the brain and the bottom one shows the compound fracture of the skull.

Celia approaching Nameless Peak. 'It needed a bolt or bravery to bypass a particularly treacherous wall, and we had neither.' January 1998.

Celia Bull, January 1998.

'I quickly attempted to climb the South Summit of Victoria Peak without a rope, solo. I looked down to find a foothold and suddenly became aware of the 3000 foot chasm below my feet.' January 1998.

'I had been a full timer, living for the rock.' Bouldering at Tapovan in the Indian Himalaya. August 1990.

people in chairs. It was like I didn't see myself as one of them. In the beginning I was still shocked and it was like I wasn't in a wheelchair and they were, but of course I was in a wheelchair. I think I'm better equipped now to take people as I see them, take them at face value, instead of thinking they've got the plague or something. Everybody should be made to visit one of these places, if only to see just how lucky they really are. There would be a lot less people feeling sorry for themselves and wasting their lives away. It would put people's petty problems into perspective.

At 7.45 of a morning the day staff arrive to relieve the night nurses. There's usually three night staff and they don't have a moment's rest, so they say. We, the patients, have no way of telling, being tucked up, fast asleep throughout the night. They don't stop changing wet, soiled sheets the whole night long, and pacifying patients' nightmares. There are a lot of them, screaming and wailing in the dead of night.

Vera Simpson, the ward sister, tells of the night's fun and games to the day staff, how so and so fell out of bed and how such and such got the fear and wailed, and from then on had a restless night. In the dead of night they watch over you with their comforting eyes, and when you do wake up you can often hear the friendly click-click-click of their heels retreating up the corridor.

Seventeen-year-old Chris acts every bit his age as he swaggers about. He's from a very deprived family and was 'pissed and whizzing' when he fell over a balcony onto concrete stairs. He's had numerous dads and was brought up in a block of flats on the Ford estate, one of the more notorious in Birkenhead. He has to get his mother to read the letters of admittance for him as he mucks about. 'My family never gave a fuck about me, so why should I fucking give a fuck about anything,' moans Chris after getting caught smoking dope in the toilets on the Unit. The neuro-psychologist is despairing of him and couldn't even wake him up for his session once. If you show no interest in helping yourself, there is less will for the therapists to help you.

21st June

Andy Cave's stag do, Midsummer's Day
In my 'sedan chair' I was carried to Earl Crag, before the bash, over muddy puddles and dangerous crevasses. I was then plonked unceremoniously on a flat rock while all the lads went bouldering. I smoked a fat fag that one of the boys has rolled me earlier and chilled out, enjoying the closing of the day. 'Looking like Ray Charles' with my shades on, someone mentioned.

We had booked rooms in the Railway Inn near Ingleton, but when I turned up in my chair the proprietor suddenly had a change of mind and told us there was no room at the inn, thereby turfing us out into the cold night and leaving us to look elsewhere. My blood boiled. How could he treat a cripple like this?

'The truth is that we aren't insured for wheelchairs,' he said apologetically. So I gave a demonstration of how mobile I was out of the chair. But 'A wheelchair's a wheelchair. It's fire regulations,' he muttered. The whole affair seemed to be discriminatory to me. But it turned out that I saved myself twenty quid and had a better night's kip in Dave Barton's van in the car park of the Hill Inn.

There was much drunken revelry. I forewent my anti-convulsants for the weekend because they make me feel extra drunk off a small amount of alcohol and extra hungover. I don't often do this, as getting pissed makes you more susceptible to fits, but I thought that just this once I'd risk it.

Climbers don't tend to tie stag night victims naked to lamp posts on the other side of the country or leave them down a back alley with their trousers round their ankles and a condom hanging out of their rectum. We did nothing horrible to Andy, we all got on with having a good time. We also tend to have women along at these stag do's, so they're not actually an all male bastion at all. Everyone's welcome.

I remember being wheeled down a steep muddy bank in the pitch darkness by a totally inebriated Mark Wright, and him losing his footing in his smooth-soled shoes, so that he was skiing, if you like, being dragged behind me. There was the flat-sided wall of a panel van down on the car park below us, but just in time he found his feet again and brought us under control.

The morning after we went en masse for a greasy fry up in Ingleton and left for the Bridestones, a collection of truly outrageous gritstone boulders of all shapes and sizes on the very top of a moor. There's one that's the exact shape of an egg that you can get rocking and one in the shape of a cow's horns. I had to be manhandled over fences and carried across tussock mogul fields. The groom-to-be fell right at the top of the Horror Arête and sprained his ankle. We all had visions of him walking to the altar in a pot leg.

After a complete traverse of Bridestones Moor the wheels of my chair were falling off. On the Monday I had to get it repaired by Nina, one of my physios, who laughed it off. She was less chuffed the time I went beach racing and, apart from the wheels dropping off, she had to clean the whole thing of sand.

22nd–26th June

The Bobath Course
I've never seen so many stroke patients in one place. It was great to witness. The patients, as long as they could walk, were in all stages of recovery. There were those that were pivoting around on a pin straight leg with their hand permanently clawing their chest. And there were those who were walking all right, apart from relying on a stick. First I had to present myself before about twenty students and show them what I could do. I walked, of sorts, for ten yards, turned, and came back to my seat. The students all made notes on my condition whilst Sharon, the chief, asked them questions that I couldn't understand. They answered in neuro-rehab speak that I couldn't understand either, all central key points and tonic, clonic whatever.

The patients then filtered into the gym and took their positions at numerous benches. Each had two physiotherapists by their side. Smithy and I were the only patients from the Neuro Rehab and had to have an ambulance booked every morning when it was time to go over to the Stroke Unit. The ambulance drivers were jealous of us being massaged by so many women and they, hilariously, pretended that their backs or shoulders were hurting them.

It was all senior physiotherapists on this course, so the quality of treatment we got as guinea pigs was far superior to any normal physio session. Plus you got two of them. I was assigned Lesley and Hanna to take me on a tour of the body, stopping at every major destination. They wasted no time targeting my hip flexor muscles as the key weak point on which to base further work.

I was totally tensing my stomach muscles whenever I wanted to kick the leg forwards. This pattern is a poor one and so I had to concentrate on moving my leg forwards without tensing my abdomen to hell. This the two women achieved through the week by a technique called prone standing. Prone standing is when you lie your top half on an electric bench, which is raised just to the height of your waist, thereby relaxing your abdomen. This leaves your hip flexor free to work without the abs kicking in. There was much more stuff than this done, but my Dictaphone was threatening to give up the ghost. Before it did I managed to get down a bit of the history of approaches to neurological rehabilitation.

Before world war two hemiplegics and other brain-injured patients would just be left to fester in bed. This led to thousands of people suffering with severe spasticity. In the early 'forties what was hailed as a great advance came about. Treatment was aimed at improving functional abilities by using the unaffected side of the hemiplegic only or concentrating on the patient's remaining abilities. This was achieved by putting a tripod stick in the patient's good hand. The goal of this treatment was to attain 'a safe but not a normal mode of travel'.

This treatment had its limitations from a functional and from an aesthetic point of view. Lots of activities are impossible without the use of both hands – opening a tin, sliced bread, grating cheese, chopping vegetables, placing protection with one hand whilst hanging onto the rock face with the other. And, of course, running, playing tennis, rock climbing and mountaineering would be impossible whilst trailing a gammy leg. The use of a tripod is now seen to be very short-sighted and, though it will aid walking in the short term, in the long term it will instil an abnormal gait pattern and so encourage spasticity.

In the late 'fifties massive steps were taken in the approaches to the rehabilitation of brain-injured patients. New physiological concepts began to be developed and in the early 'sixties Bertie Bobath was to the fore of these. Originally looking for a treatment for cerebral palsied children, she made use of the facilitation of 'normal postural reflex activity'. This isn't as complicated as it sounds and basically means the trunk providing a base for normal movement and the limbs following.

Once the therapist gets the 'central key point', the trunk, as a stable base from which to work the rest should, but doesn't always, fall into line. It depends on the amount of damage inflicted to the brain. The other key points are the proximal, the limbs. In the rehabilitation of hemiplegics lots of emphasis is placed on the correct alignment of the key points of a particular postural set, be it sitting or standing. The relief of spasticity, plenty of stretching, is an important part of therapy also.

Bertie Bobath trained at the Berlin school for gymnastics study-ing the analysis of movement. It was the 1930s and Nazism was getting its ugly claws into Germany. In 1938 she fled Germany for London where she married Karel Bobath, himself an eminent physiologist who was born in Eastern Europe. They worked together to develop a new form of physiotherapy which was, unfortunately, ahead of the physiological thinking of the time. Their followers had difficulty finding acceptance amongst the staid proponents of the old school. Eventually, though, they found credibility and now their art, for physiotherapy is an art, is practised in all the corners of the world.

Obviously some techniques have been superseded and other disciplines, such as the Peto technique from Hungary, have come about. Ways of thinking have progressed enormously but the name Bobath is still well respected. In the early 'nineties, when in old age, the couple passed away quietly together.

28th June

I glide silently through corridors in my wheelchair with only the tap-tap of my one foot, which propels me.

A scream. I can tell it's Friday morning by that scream. Kevin is taking his weekly shower before the ambulance comes to take him home. Being scrubbed down by nurses in the most intimate places, his shouts go from a low rumble to a high-pitched squeal in one loud swear. He appears, looking smart in his new blue shell suit, with his ginger hair all washed and fluffy.

In the courtyard, with the warmth of the sun on my face, I close my eyes and feel the orange heat on my lids. It takes me back to a million places all at once, sitting on some dirty hotel's roof in Delhi, hanging belayed to rivets in the midnight sun on Mount Asgard, the brutal heat on the Baltoro Glacier in Pakistan, or simply to my beloved hills, lying in the grass where I can sniff its sweet scent below a crag in Wales.

30th June

The ambulance came just as Celia was dyeing my hair (pillar box red). Very embarrassing. I had to hold up the two ambulance men and two other patients while I rinsed it out. We were going to Walton for an ECG. I met this very pleasant bald-headed technician who explained everything that he was doing very well. He put twenty monitors equidistant around my head with a sodium chloride gel to get rid of dead skin and two heart-rate monitors on the backs of my wrists. I asked him to turn the computer screen around so that I could see it also. With my eyes open the screen resembled the numerous false horizons you see on hazy days in the mountains, all spikes and deep valleys. If I shut them and open them quickly the input into my brain looked like the Himalaya through the screen. I came back on my own with the ambulance men and, there not being old people to offend, they got off on listening to some rowdy American comedian called Bill Hicks.

England was put out of the World Cup today on a penalty shoot out. They were down to ten men as Beckham was sent off for tapping an Argentinian player on the back of the leg with his boot. It was two goals all when Shearer fouled the goalkeeper just as Leseax put it in the back of the net. The goal was disallowed and so with all the time out it went to thirty minutes' extra time and the golden goal ruling. England put up an incredible fight, down to ten men, and the final whistle blew. They lost on penalties.

My last accident got my mum and my dad talking, on the telephone, for the first time since their marriage break-up seventeen years ago. Usually every negative event carries something positive along with it. This accident was no different.

I'd had a fall on Creagh Meaghaidh, ice climbing in winter. Two hundred feet I went, on to a poor ice screw, crampons and axes flailing as I cartwheeled backwards through clean air. I was working as a guide at the time and felt a guilt I had never experienced before or since. I had become over-ambitious, which is dodgy when you're with your climbing partner, never mind people who are paying you to work for them.

My clients Robert and Nick were excellent though. Robert was a doctor and so gave me an on the spot diagnosis. He said that I'd broken my back and that my difficulty breathing was probably due to a broken sternum. Nick Kikus, a very experienced guide working for the same company as myself, happened to be following me up the route. He had two clients also, so had to lower the five of us down the gully for 1000 feet. The gully bed wrecked my back with every undulation, and when I was lowered down the numerous small cliffs the pain was so intense I feared I was going to pass out. My vertebrae were like a pig iron chain being pulled over a right-angled edge. This went on rope-length after rope-length. Nick tied the ropes end to end to lower us twice as quickly.

We hit the avalanche fan and I couldn't untie the knot. I had debilitating pain in my back and chest. I teetered around, my back feeling hinged, and walked down to a flat spot, were the helicopter would be able to pick me up. I then lay down flat on my back with my legs bent and cried. Nick's Dutch clients didn't know what to make of me and kept their distance.

The guys went in search of the mountain rescue box and after some trouble, due to map-reading, they found it. I soon had blankets piled on top of me and a surgical collar on my neck. Then the clients slogged back the six miles through the snow to call out the rescue team from some bar or other at dusk, while I lay there waiting to hear the throbbing of rotor blades.

I asked Nick if he had ever had any similar experiences, treading very carefully, because I knew that he had but never spoke about it. He started to talk slowly and deliberately about how his good friend and climbing partner had fallen near the top of a Himalayan peak. 'There was only the two of us that time, going fast and light, alpine-style. He smashed his head up and I had to lower him 3000 feet to the bottom of the mountain.' His friend was dead when they reached the foot of the face.

I remember saying something about being scared to die, not because of the pain of it. I knew it wasn't painful. But because I was sure there was nothing afterwards. No life after death. I felt I had proved that to myself in my earlier drowning incident on Wen Zawn.

The helicopter's whirring blades cut through the night air as it approached. I remember seeing the spot lights, two or three of them sweeping the snow, and thinking this is just like *Close Encounters of the Third Kind*, when the alien space craft lands on Devil's Tower. Out climbed strange faces that were ruthlessly efficient. I remember extreme discomfort as one of them fitted the surgical collar more professionally to my neck.

The Lochaber rescue team loaded me up; I knew one of them and had a brief chat with him before the oxygen mask was planted over my nose and mouth. The ride was draughty but before I knew it we had landed at Fort William in Safeway's car park. There was no room at the hospital for a helipad so we were transferred into an ambulance to be driven the remaining hundred yards.

In Accident and Emergency I was dazzled by the light and lay there not caring that a strapping female nurse was snipping my clothes off me with scissors – my Gore-Tex jacket and salopettes, my Windstopper jacket and salopettes and finally my thermal underwear top and bottoms. I lay there naked apart from my neck brace until the warm towels came and covered me. I was so cold that they could have been at room temperature, but they still felt hot to me. Then it was a trolley ride with two orderlies in blue trousers and white shirts down to the x-ray department. The x-rays revealed four broken vertebrae, a broken sternum and a fractured right orbit. I had a haemorrhaged right eyeball into the bargain as well, which was a deep red.

If that accident was the first time my mum and dad had talked, this most recent accident was the first time I had seen my parents together for eighteen years. I studied them for signs of affection but, apart from a peck on the cheek, they just behaved like good friends. I couldn't believe that two people so different could find themselves together and married for twenty-four years.

It was the first time I'd seen my dad since the accident and the only time he's been to the Rehab Unit or the hospital. He felt uncomfortable with the Unit and my friends, whom he hadn't before met. Celia's sister, Elaine, was there and my mother happened to mention my painted toenails. Now my dad is a working-class man in every respect, apart from his doctrine of not working if you can help it, with very traditional views. He started on a rant as only my dad can. 'A man's got to dress like a man,' and 'Only jungle bunnies wear that stuff on their nails.' I cringed with embarrassment in front of Elaine. My mum had heard it all before. That is essentially why she divorced him.

I knew from past experience that to challenge him would be a bad idea and that there would be no knowing what he could do then – rant and rave in front of the other patients on the ward or feign a heart attack, as he'd once done with my brother, or end up threatening a nurse, which was always a possibility.

Don't get me wrong though, he was a great dad, who had plenty of time for us kids. We played footie every evening and he would take us on fishing holidays and weekends, too. He would take my brother and me shooting also, shotguns at the ready as we stalked down dawn meadows hunting rabbits or anything that moved.

He took us to Spain all through the winter months which is how we missed most of our education. We would just go swimming in the Mediterranean or messing around in half-built apartment blocks. My dad made enough money as a property repairer (that's what he liked to be known as) in the summer to keep us comfortably off in Spain for the winter. He kept us away from school on hot summer days and that suited us down to the ground. The final straw for my mum was when he went to Spain for four months, taking David with him, and didn't tell my mother anything about it. She didn't want to go because she wanted at least some semblance of an education for my sister Tracey and me. It was too late for David, he was already sixteen and in line for the building trade – 'Bugger O levels.'

4th July

Simon and Jane's wedding

Ali picked me up from my mum's house and we hurtled up the M6, knowing that we were late. We arrived at Great Salkeld church after the service had started. You can just slip in unnoticed if you are on foot but in a wheelchair, not so. When the door opened the commotion created by entering the church meant all eyes were on us. Once all eyes were on us then it was time to roll over the door curtain in the chair and rip it down. A very embarrassing entry.

I stood up to sing hymns and outside after the service, there were lots of folk I hadn't seen for ages who wanted, naturally, to know how I was doing and all about the accident. This gets a bit tiresome, but they can't help it. It's not their fault. It's their only point of reference, the only thing they know what to talk about with you. Being in hospital, you have been out of the scene so long.

I can now sympathise with Simon Yates who works as a guide, climbing mountains in the Himalaya and the former Soviet Union. He's away from home for perhaps seven months of the year and complains about how no one talks to him any more about anything other than his work. They perceive it to be fascinating and can only dream of standing on his summits. But he would much rather be in his garden and spend his time talking about vegetables.

5th July

I dreamt that I stretched my fingers out last night, I just straightened them, that was it, and it was so real that I don't know whether it happened or not. I woke myself up in the excitement of it all, pulled my hand from under the sheet and tried desperately to repeat the movement. I strained and strained but all the straining seemed to be coming from my abdominal muscles. It's like that, you use what muscles you can use and then suddenly, one day, you remember how to use the appropriate muscles and *voilà*. You're away. Ever so weakly away, but there's movement nevertheless. And you might again forget how to use the limb, but you can be confident that you'll remember how it works once more.

6th July

Paper clip as opposed to safety pin, spice jar, cotton bobbin, ball bearing as opposed to marble, bottle washer, nut and bolt, clothes peg, wooden ball, table tennis ball, big and small padlock, Yale key and mortice lock, darts case and all other manner of items. Today in the occupational therapy I had to identify numerous objects by touch with my eyes closed. This is easier said than done. When you can't manipulate an object in your hand, run it between your fingers, check out whether it's got any moving parts, and your hand is totally numb, but is getting less so by the day. I have to have Lise do the hand manipulating for me. Lise is Norwegian, from a little village near Stavanger and her accent is charming, in a high-pitched sort of way. My hand's getting more sensation in it all the time.

Last night I wheeled up to Andrew's table for dinner and asked him how he was. He answered, 'I'd be OK if you'd stop banging my table.' And then went into a repetitive rant. 'I would be if you'd stop banging my table. I would be if you stop banging my table. I would be if you stopped banging my table. I would be if you stop. I would be if you. I would be. I would be.'

And he was off into his horse race commentator mode again. You felt extremely sorry for him but even the nurses can't suppress a giggle when he kicks off, faster and faster, more and more garbled.

7th July

I can hear him screaming in a single ward they keep for the disturbed, whenever the nurses go round to give the guy with the bush baby eyes his injections. His screams echo down the corridor in the darkness as if he's being tortured. He was being wheeled about today and he told me that you must never give up fighting and that you will get there in the end.

The doctors told him he would never walk again and he says he told them 'politely to eff off, politely where to stick it.' He was a determined sort who kept saying splendid. He had been in the army in Northern Ireland and though he kept on repeating himself he was a friendly lad. 'I'm getting there slowly but surely' he would persistently declare. 'I'm not bragging or anythin' but I used to be a right nutter.' He will be squirming in agony saying that his leg is in a lot of pain and the nurses, who know best, will just leave him be. I will have to go back to my writing because it is unbearable to see a man in such pain, even if it is in his imagination. As he is wheeled back down the corridor I can hear him telling the nurse the story of how six blokes set about him with baseball bats.

His wrist was bent forwards, set permanently at a right angle. Both the tops of his feet were in line with his shinbones. But, far worse than these injuries, he had a shocking memory. You can do creative things, like write a book, if your brain is functioning vaguely correctly but if it isn't and you can't even see the problem, that is where the really sad cases of the neuro scene are. Imagine not being able to motivate yourself to get better because you're not even aware that anything is the matter with you.

But it isn't all sadness. There is some degree of hope in nearly all these cases. (I say nearly all because there isn't such a luxury for MS patients, only remission.) But I have seen completely mangled guys with a mental age of seven, incontinent, wheelchair-bound and completely disinhibited, come through here. And when they leave they're in a much better state. Not totally recovered but far healthier.

10th July

I had a new patient in the bed opposite who was very confused and displaced. He had a head as bald as a cue ball and those glasses that make your eyes seem way bigger than they actually are. He kept shouting to an imaginary dog called Sam in the middle of the night. 'Get 'em, Sam. Who's there, Sam?' Cue Ball's bed had to be wheeled out into the day room at 5.30 a.m. because he kept us awake all night. He decided to perform a strip in the day room yesterday evening. Off came his shirt, his shoes, then his tracky bottoms and, finally, his underpants. The nurses fought with him but it was to no avail. Short of restraining him by tying his arms to the arms of the chair, which I'm sure the social worker would have a problem with, there was nothing they could do. So he was strapped in to the padded wheelchair, as he is always, and put up quite a struggle.

Because Smithy, young Chris and I all had head injuries it would take only the slightest thing to set us off hysterically laughing. I awoke from a deep sleep to see the Cue Ball naked on the floor. He'd somehow dismantled his cot sides and crawled out, head- or feet-first, I don't know, and was lying like an overturned beetle, legs and arms flailing. The others woke up too, after some prompting, and we got the giggles just like you do when you're kids. I rang the bell and the nurse came in bewildered, saying, 'He must have a degree in engineering or a tool kit in his bed to unbolt that cot side.'

I moved my arm today about eight inches in abduction and there was activity in my tricep, the first we've seen. It's wild stuff this neuro-plasticity thing. After three months of Lise constantly facilitating my arm, polishing the table or picking up cones and placing them down again, or dropping them, I now have movement. Not much, admittedly, but where there's life, that activity can only get stronger. That has been my constant motto.

13th July

I went to a rave at the weekend. I had dinner with Charlie and then we went partying. We went up this winding track to a dam and there were a hundred cars lining the road, and two home-made marquees. There were generators and cables and fire dancers at 3 a.m. I was carried and pushed over open moorland to the marquee were I started to dance. There were some fantastic dancers there, and then there was me. Using only one arm to dance with I got some very strange looks, especially off the policemen who came to have a whip round for the farmer whose land we were on. 'How did the bloke in the wheelchair get up here?' I heard one of them say.

My legs started to shake as I danced the night away. I was moving my hips, too. My right arm was swinging limp and I was on rigid legs, though I did manage to bend them, slightly, as I got into the groove. It was like my legs were trying to dance without me doing anything about it. They were shaking roughly in time to the throbbing beat of the music as if they had some innate sense of rhythm. The heels were lifting uncontrollably and I would have to sit down for a spell in my wheelchair, which I had strategically positioned right behind me.

I watched the murky dawning in the pissing rain and was furiously happy to be alive. We drove back home, my head out of the car window, soaking up the beginning of the day and listening to 'Whole Lotta Love' by Lead Zeppelin, played loud.

When I got back to the Unit on Monday morning my body was in tatters. Associated reactions all over the place. My arm was bent in a permanent right angle, my hand was clenched in a fist, my wrist was flexed, very spastic, and the leg kept standing on tiptoe. I felt like Victor Hugo's Hunchback. In one evening I had ruined all the good work that Jill and Tricia and Gulhan, the physiotherapists, had done.

There is lots of frivolity on the ward today, nurses hassling each other in a friendly way, gossiping intensely. Brenda's the main culprit, and Pauline's a fairly keen gossip as well. The whole of the UK is divided into Scousers and Woolly Backs. Paul's the only real Scouser here; the rest of us are Woolly Backs. That is the not too affectionate term for anyone outside Liverpool. Jenny, a pencil-thin kick-boxer who won her first fight against a woman who was training for England, threw water over Liz. Liz, who must be three times the size of Jenny, meant to retaliate but just as she'd filled up the water jug again and Jenny was hiding behind a curtain with only her face poking out, Vera, the ward manager, appeared and thwarted her attempt.

You have to laugh in a place like this; otherwise you'd go off your trolley. It seems cruel to laugh at the patients but you have to see the humour in it and anyway I am a patient. I am one of them. How can I laugh at myself if I can't laugh at the others around me? The nurses have a good laugh at the patients' expense, too, but they are laughing with them, not at them.

I am now approaching the six-month watershed in my recovery. The first six months are the time when the docs say the most intense period of recovery will happen. After that it will be a slow uphill struggle for the next two and a half years and then it should plateau out for good. There will be little plateaus all through my recovery and I have already experienced them from time to time. When seemingly nothing happens for three weeks to a month you start to get worried off your head and you start to think that that's it, you won't get any better. Then suddenly, out of nowhere, some movement happens and you get all excited for a few days. In fact, it is a really exciting time for me at this moment. It's not every day you get the use of a limb.

So I'm willing my fingers like mad to get them working, but they always end up going into flexion instead of extension. Flexion is the movement I've already got; it's the stretch and the extension

I need. It's the same with my elbow and wrist. I can pull them inwards, like I'm curling, but there's no straightening to be done.

Lise is working on soothing my over-tight muscles, teaching them how to relax. If my tendons and muscles are too tensed in my flexors, my bicep and forearm, she asks how can my extensor muscles stand a chance, fighting against that?

15th July

The nurses are preparing for the annual barbecue. Shifting rubbish that has been accumulating over the year, rotting tables and parasols that have woodlice under them. The primary nurse is filling up the pond and the orderlies are sweeping the patio and throwing bed sheets over the tables to make them look better. A completely spherical fellow lit the barbecue with lighter fuel.

When 7.30 arrived it was out with the tinnies and in with the feeding frenzy. Kids played football, there was a Brazilian team and a French team, they also fished for ducks in the pond, played the tombola and ate lots. The adults got steadily pissed and there was a certain disregard for the drugs they were on by the nurses. Smithy bought Kevin a pint of ale, which he didn't touch. There were wheelchairs everywhere, a right traffic jam at times. I couldn't get to the hatch where the beer was coming from and had to ask our ward manager's daughter to bring it to me.

Smithy's daughter excelled at the tombola and, amidst all the cuddly toys and porcelain ornaments, she won three bottles of booze for us. Smithy made short work of the whisky and started telling stories of how when he had the catheter removed the first piss he had was like 'the longest cum I've ever done'. He also told me the story about when 'the boys' came into hospital 'with a tin of Special Brew and a pipe packed full of grass'. It was only a month after his car smash. So he lay there drinking his beer through a straw and smoking his pipe. The smoke quickly filled the ward and just as quickly 'the boys' were ushered out of the hospital and told not to come back. He looked like Charlie Chaplin with his stick as he walked down the corridor, drunk, later that night. I stayed up after all the other patients went to bed and had a crack with four nurses who told me all sorts of gossip. The only bit that comes to mind is about one very large nurse who must weigh twenty stones. She is the kindest and most selfless nurse on the unit and they assured me she ballet dances in a pink tutu. Aren't you supposed to believe everything a nurse tells you?

18th July

At the weekend I went to a house party. I made an entrance on my feet. I walked up the steps to the front door, opened it, and walked through. There were about ten good friends there and two strangers. One stranger had a skinhead with dreadlocks hanging off the back and homemade tattoos all the way up his arms – things like 'I HATE MY MUM' on his forearm and 'H-A-T-E' and 'H-A-T-E' on each knuckle. He had a hook-nose, a stubbly sharp chin and the look of an archetypal escaped psychiatric patient.

This evil-looking character grabbed my wheelchair and placed it down. This was a kindly enough action and he wasn't to know any different when he started pulling my right arm to guide me into it, but my arm was cripplingly painful and, in his lashed up state, he pulled it too hard. I gave out a cry and shouted, 'Leave it alone, will you.' Not meaning to cause offence, it was just the pain.

As soon as I'd sat in my chair he set about me, hitting me hard about the head. My instinct was to protect the hole in my head and I curled up with my hands on the top of my skull. He was dragged off only after he had got three or four blows in and my friends stood around me as a shield. I was then ejected out of the back door and into the potting shed where I had to calm myself by smoking something herbal.

It was the first time the hole in my head had been threatened and I felt very vulnerable. I felt vulnerable also because, in my wheelchair, I couldn't retaliate. This made me angry to the point at which I could hardly stop shaking. Violence has never been a big thing with me but if I saw a guy in a wheelchair getting punched I wouldn't be able to help myself. In my fury I would attack. I had to quell my anger because there was absolutely nothing I could do about it. I could hardly stand up and say, 'Unhand me you ruffian or I'll punch your lights out.'

21st July

Went to Liverpool for a CT scan today or a computed tomography scan. Some people call them Cat scans. I was led down this corridor at the new wing of the Fazakerley Hospital, all stacked high with boxes and building materials. A mountain of a woman then led me into the treatment room, which was hardly finished, and I was the first patient to be treated there. They were still taping the lead to the windows. And then I was placed in this giant polo mint thing which zaps x-rays at you and builds up an image of your head in slices.

When I got the results back from my ECG they were fairly typical of someone who has suffered head trauma – irregular electric currents and wave patterns.

23rd July

A real breakthrough today. I held my tricep in tension for a full thirty seconds and even moved it throughout its full range. I was lying down and Trish held my arm vertically. She then let go and I held my own arm up for thirty seconds. When I relaxed it, the arm lowered down toward my chest and then, the most important point, I managed to isolate and tense my tricep, thereby extending my arm out again.

I'll miss Smithy when he goes; next week, he says. He has a knife-sharp wit on him and can make anyone smile. He got seventy year-old Kay laughing, and she looked at death's door. A crackhead who admits, 'I'm addicted to the rock,' Smithy has no teeth and a deep scar down the middle of his forehead. He loves drugs, I mean really loves them. He talks in a language I barely know of Peruvian flake, bars and keys.

There were probably three times during his stay here when I didn't see him smiling. That's when the psychotic Smithy appears. The seriously depressed Smithy. He's best left well alone when he's like that. I never saw him turn tables upside down or wreck the day room but I'm sure he was capable of it and it would have got a thing or two off his chest. More often than not, though, you would see the grin through that woolly beard, a monkey in a bush.

Cue Ball was hysterical tonight. Whenever you mention him getting all the attention off the nurses he breaks into a broad grin. He knows what he's up to. He even called Vera, the ward manager, a loose woman.

I cooked a spinach and tofu curry for lunch in occupational therapy and all the nurses had some. I miss cooking desperately. The preparation of food is very therapeutic – peeling, chopping and slicing, cracking eggs, adding spices well ground in a mortar and pestle, the sizzle as you add raw onion to hot oil. I got to cook two lunches a week in the OT kitchen but that wasn't enough. I wanted to cook every day. I started by cooking pasta pesto and graduated to lentil dahl. Now I'm making such varied delights as tofu and coriander Taiwanese-style, caldo verde or banana sponge.

It's not easy preparing food with only your left hand. I rely on tools such as the one-handed electric can-opener, the spiked chopping board and the rocker knife, as well as low surfaces, sink and cooker. The food I've had the most difficulty with is chopping and pressing garlic. When I chop it, it is liable to go all over the floor and when I use the press my right arm comes all the way up into the archetypal spastic position. But I find that there is a solution to every problem.

25th July

A day trip to Dublin today with the Llanberis gang, Charlie, Sonic Sue, Chris Rhys and the Lentil. The Lentil began his life in Llanberis at Tydyn Sian, the Lentil Farm – a rather derogatory name for the local conservationists' dwelling. We had set out with the idea to visit galleries but soon, or rather I should say, as soon as we got off the boat, it degenerated into a drinking and shopping trip. With considerably more of the former.

I learnt a thing or two about the lateral stability of my chair, and the Lentil saved me from a certain spilling when I tried to mount a kerb and it didn't work. I was just about to give myself another head injury when the chair tipped over to the right. I couldn't have put my hand out to stop my face planting itself on the paving, but the Lentil, who must have been ten yards away at the time, sprinted and just caught me.

Then there was the struggle to find a pub to eat at where you didn't have to walk up stairs. We failed on that score and I fought my way upstairs in one bar, looking like Bela Lugosi, and almost nose-dived straight into a diner's lap. A friend who we met in a climbing shop by the River Liffy pointed us to the Zanzibar, which was a bit tacky but great for wheeling around in, and it even had wheelchair-accessible toilets.

There was a group of English and a group of Welsh on stag days enjoying misbehaving. On the train on the way back Sonic had to lend one of them her nail varnish. He painted a bright purple cross on the forehead of a man who was in the most paralytic stupor. The Welsh pissheads were more friendly than the English pissheads, who seemed to us to be rather sinister.

On the return crossing I met a friend I hadn't seen since childhood. He hadn't changed a bit, though now he was playing football professionally. He always had something that none of the rest of us had. He tackled with a definite style and passed the ball spot on. When he left school he went to play for Bolton Wanderers and had since been to Oxford and Middlesbrough. I suddenly felt like that little boy again. Jimmy was a year or two older than I was and always cast that boyhood spell. Me being down in my chair and him standing above me only served to revive and accentuate my childhood feeling of inferiority to this Adonis, this footballing hero. I felt like a real cripple next to this giant.

In reality he stood no taller than I did, but I had been sitting down for half a year and had learnt to see the world from this perspective. I had grown accustomed to viewing everyone's bums in the pub and on the dance floor. Yeah, I felt like a cripple because that was what I was next to this paragon of health. No matter how much people tried to humour me, that is how I saw myself. I wheeled away angry, not with him, though that wasn't apparent at first, but with myself for being so weak.

It is an unusual fact that all people in wheelchairs are drunk magnets. All the drunks from miles around home in on the wheelchair user and, with genuine sympathy on their faces, ask if you are OK or if you need any help. If you needed help you would have asked for it and anyway, if your idea of help is being hauled up a flight of stairs by a pissed up punter, risking severe injury, when in reality you were trying to cross the road, then you're welcome to it.

Dublin was no exception. This awful bloke started to breathe on me and fondle my leg, asking in slurred English, again and again, if I was OK. I said, 'Yes, of course I was fucking OK. Why shouldn't I be?' And my outburst surprised me.

When we got back to Holyhead I was dying for a piss and waited outside one of the accessible toilets with an engaged sign on the door. It was funny because I usually am aware of the other passengers in wheelchairs and I hadn't seen any at all. Eventually the door unlocked and out walked one of the Welsh team with a big fat spliff. We giggled at how the accessible toilets have their uses for everyone.

27th July

I was held under suspicion today in the WRVS shop. There was a guy in charge who I heard whispering to one of the women, 'Keep your eye on him.' I took offence and I asked him outright if he thought I was a shoplifter and what led him to come to his conclusion. Was it the Red Chilli hair colour or the emerald toe nails or the unshaven face because I'd forgotten my shaver? I got an apology out of the guy, which was all I was after. I'm sure he thought he would have a dangerous psycho wreaking havoc in his shop if he didn't apologise.

29th July

'I'll meet you on top of Everest before I'll work within a year,' spluttered Smithy. 'The neuro woman says I'll be working again in a year. I need at least two years off to get me head together. When I came out of that coma the doctors said I'd be all right. Lying bastards,' he laughs, spraying his beer all over me.

Tom, who I never got to know very well during my whole stay at Clatterbridge, came over and spoke with us. He garbled like a mad man about his whole experience but he owned up to driving a motorbike. He had never done that before. He had always said he'd been in a car when he hit that bollard in Jamaica.

Kathy, baby Angel and Philippa took me on a 'family day out' to the Tate Gallery in Liverpool today. Amidst the half-sunken boat 'SOS 1998', and the pile of mint Imperials, 'Portrait of Dad 1991', there was a Picasso entitled 'Seated Nude' which I stared at for ages, not knowing why, and then it became apparent. I saw myself in there. The male figure was seated, as I am, but also had its arms twisted into the spastic position, knuckles facing up, wrist bent up and forearm turned in as if in a sling. The Cubist painting was built up of triangles and had no right side to the face, as I didn't have once. One ghostly eye was staring; the right side of its mouth was drooping at a horrible slant. Its right bicep was totally flat and without definition, but its trapezium and lats were working overtime.

The only difference was he was holding something tenderly, a baby perhaps or something more peculiar, to his chest. I couldn't have held anything tenderly if I'd tried. My hand is still clenched into a permanent fist unless I concentrate on relaxing for about a minute beforehand. Maybe he was releasing a bird? There were its wings. It stirred in me a sense of immediate hope. He came out from his background, a mosaic of browns through greys, and started to wheel towards me. I stood back and made way for him, as his chair rolled. I had always appreciated art, but now I craved it. I saw myself staring at simple objects, appreciating their simplicity.

It's the simple things I miss – hugging someone when they're feeling down. To do that you have to be on your feet with both arms working. I miss being hugged when I'm feeling down, too, and not feeling infantile because of being at a lower level. And there's scratching your left arm or picking flowers on your knees in a summer meadow.

31st July

I got drunk in the pub, just like my South East Asian consultant told me not to. She said that at Simon and Jane's wedding, not wanting to be a total killjoy, I could toast the bride. If she could see me now she would shake her head and say simply I told you so. I know drinking alcohol can greatly increase the risk of seizure, but it's my risk. Hell, you've got to have some fun and take a few risks. As far as I'm concerned that's what life's about, taking risks.

After six months you get a bit bored with trying to be a goody two shoes all the time.

I walked into this party with my spotter, Leigh McGinley, who was definitely more pissed than I was. I need a spotter when I'm walking, especially when I'm walking drunk. Anyway, he totally missed me keeling over; he was looking in the other direction. I slammed down hard, crossways, onto a chair with wooden arms and took a blow to my jaw and elbow. Obviously it didn't hurt at the time, due to the anaesthetic effect of the drink, but when I awoke it took me a while to realise why my jaw was killing me. Then I vomited.

1st August

Charlie and Sonic Sue had a very fine barbecue with heaps of meat to celebrate the Lentil's birthday. I spent most of the time in the kitchen listening to Smoo playing his harp. I was overawed to hear him play a rendition of 'Old McDonald Had a Farm', which is tantamount to sacrilege on such a delicate instrument.

Merlin then wheeled me home down a ridiculously steep hill at 2 a.m. When a motor car stopped to say good evening my chauffeur started to experience raging paranoia. The driver was dressed in a black suit and was only trying to be helpful, but Merlin clammed up and left me to do the answering. Afterwards he declared, 'It's the DS. I'm sure of it. Why else would "a suit" be driving around this late at night?' All the while I was striking matches to illuminate the road ahead.

3rd August

A new patient came onto the ward today. Chaz is a veritable ball of a man at twenty stone who had his car accident back in 1962. And he is still having treatment for it! He's a real joker but I can't quite put my finger on it, his jokes don't always make sense. He asked me if my new-fangled computer can make my fingers longer. I pondered on this for a while, not wanting to negate the old man's ideas, but finally gave up and asked him what he had meant. He answered with a bizarre series of hand signals, which led me to believe the crash had left him a few shillings short of a pound. But as happy as a pig in shit. He walks with an appalling limp aided with a stick.

Chaz was in a coma for three months and can't remember anything about the preceding year. He says the saddest thing of the whole affair was that he took away a girl's virginity and can't remember anything of it. Nothing at all.

He passed me a piece of cheese this suppertime that he had been saving since tea. But it was all soft and warm and unappetising and I put it down the side of my seat when he wasn't looking. Then he posed the question, 'Do they swear in heaven?' He looked at me and laughed when he saw I had no idea. He answered with another question, 'Do they fuckin' hell?' and proceeded to break down into hysterical laughter.

He fell over this evening and it took three nurses and a hell of a commotion to lift him. Then he sat, all hippopotamus-like, looking dejected on the end of his bed. Sleep evaded me as the ward commenced to vibrate with the almighty racket of his pneumatic snore. I tried to sleep for three and a half hours before I saw that I just had to move wards. Once as far away from him as I possibly could be, his snores were just distant echoes and I slept with my usual soundness.

It's scary seeing in Chaz what I could end up like. Of course I'm more mentally together than he is but physically he's a mess. I'm not going to end up overweight like him if I can help it, but the stiff-legged bit I can do without. The only hope for me is that he has his hand working, but weakly. Nevertheless it is a functioning hand.

Chaz has such a dreadful limp and pivots around on a stick because he had dated methods of rehabilitation. He was one of the ones that used to walk with a tripod. He can't ride a bicycle or go rock climbing, as I hope to one day, but he can cut bread and take lids off bottles, things that I can't do yet.

4th August

When you raise your right leg or arm you only use the left hemisphere of your brain and vice versa. But because it takes so much concentration to move my over-weak limbs I am using the right hemisphere also. This does not mean that my plastic brain is learning to use both hemispheres to move one side of my body. It just means that I'm cognitively processing the movement of my right side, instead of it just happening as a reflex.

5th August

I was having a chat with Chaz this evening and he began telling me about how he couldn't get it up any more. He told me about how they put him in a room with his wife and they were made to watch pornographic movies together. It didn't work though. He said I had twenty-nine years to go before 'the greatest pleasure known to man' would be taken away from me. I suggested letting Smithy get hold of some Viagra for him. Smithy can get hold of Blue Niagaras for twenty-five quid a go. Chaz is much more lucid than I first thought and I had an intelligent, if somewhat rude, conversation with him. We also chatted about all the places we've been, him sailing me climbing.

I had a toe wiggle this morning, the first for two months. It was great, better than the swelling and I couldn't wait to tell Trish and Gulhan about it. I was able to flex and extend my elbow, under controlled conditions, in physio today. That may not sound like much but believe you me it took an immense amount of effort.

Caroline Young, my consultant neurologist, deliberately tried to get me to blush this afternoon. And she succeeded. She asked me what I had to think about to get my arm to rise in an associated reaction. I didn't say anything. She then asked if it was dirty and told me all the dirty jokes she knew were too rude for me. I replied, 'Try me.'

7th August

It's a Friday. I go home every Friday. I cherish my weekends at home. You have company twenty-four hours a day in this place. So it's good to go home for some solitude, although the guys often have 'entertainment' laid on for me, like going to the boozer or taking me to watch them climbing. I will make myself a brew, put some Nusrat Fateh Ali Khan or Shostakovich on the CD and sit in an armchair, out on the veranda if the sun is shining, and just relax. Soaking up the solitude. Revelling in the aloneness of it all.

10th August

I went to Trev's birthday party this weekend. Trev's one of my oldest friends and climbing companions. Emily, Trev's partner, carried me up a flight of steps at 5 a.m. She's muscular with long flowing black hair, a real Amazon. They're probably the craziest couple in Llanberis.

I also went to dinner with a few new friends. I find I get bored with the climbing gossip these days. I don't have any interest in the handholds of the Cad as they're mimed out in front of me. I don't see any more reason to listen to the 'numbers on Tufty Club Rebellion'. When I'm taken to sit in my chair below a cliff all I feel is jealousy, jealousy at what they're doing, flexing and stretching as they make fun of me, saying with their movement, look at me. Look how special I am, as I do the splits, mocking me with the fluidity of their gyrations, as they contort into ever more wonderful positions.

So I don't see why I should hang out with a group of intense climbers now. It's a challenge to get to know new people as well. It takes considerably more effort hanging out with comparative strangers than with your good friends, so it could be construed as therapy. Don't get me wrong. I still have my hardcore friends who will always be there for me and I for them. No, it's the acquaintances whose only point of reference with me is climbing, they're the ones who bore me in a crowded pub, as I can't even escape because of this damn wheelchair.

12th August

I visited the Tate again today because I just had to see the Picasso again. This time he looked like a woman and she is still how I feel.

I have figured out why my foot is shaking violently whenever I try to walk on it, or at least my physiotherapist has discovered why. Apparently the planta muscles on the arch of my foot are extremely tight and the only way to stretch them out is by walking on the foot as much as possible. But still only under controlled supervision.

13th August

A special day. Six months exactly since my injury. It feels distinctly odd to have come up against the six-month wall. They say that the most prolific recovery goes on in the first six months and then it slows down after that. I'm worried that it will be downhill from now on.

Tricia put my mind at rest. 'Obviously a therapist would include sitting up and turning from shoulder to shoulder in bed as recovery in the first six months.' So I have come a long way. A hell of a long way. Lying there in my hospital bed, wishing they would amputate my limbs, calling out loud for them to amputate my leg, I do realise how far I've come, and I remember what she has told me about the plateaus when nothing is happening and the excitement when a muscle begins to tense or a tendon will start twitching. The emotional intensity every time I get something back is overwhelming.

They had a goal-planning meeting without me the other day. It was decided that I could completely take care of myself, what with self-medicating and preparing food, and so they thought that I could do my own washing and drying on the line and make my own bed. Just as long as they don't expect any hospital corners from me.

The nurses, Julie, Mo and Irene, are buzzing round the ward this morning, getting the patients up who are unable to get themselves up, making beds, one on each side, with a surgeon's precision, while Liz the domestic in her pink dress sweeps and mops the floor.

Julie, a slight, pretty nurse, is shaving Cue Ball. I can hear the peaceful sound of the razor swishing through the soapy water and her soft voice humming nondescript tunes, the chat about Preston North End and teeth-cleaning. The flat feet of Ann clopping down the corridor, leaning as if she's about to fall over; the click-clack of doors as they are opened and closed; even the wailing of Kevin or the mantras of Andrew, the distant screaming of Marty or the thrashing of Cue Ball on this peaceful morning, I shall miss when I leave this place.

17th August

My step-sister Geraldine married this weekend. That was the reason I had my hair dyed purple. I wanted to show them that I still had control over my life, even if it was only over my hair.

During the wedding disco I longed to be up there dancing. It didn't matter that the music wasn't my scene, I just had an overwhelming urge to dance. But I felt like an outsider amidst all the beautiful people. I had no reason to feel this, except for paranoia. I chatted to lots of people but the conversation always came back round to the wheelchair and why I was in it. But just as soon as I was in the depths of my paranoid state, an attractive woman offered to dance with me. We kind of danced for maybe five tracks, she on her feet and me sitting, before she took her leave.

I felt suffocated by love this weekend. I know they are all worried about me, my mother, sisters and brothers. My mother, it seemed, would not take her eye off me. But she had been through it, though never quite this bad, twice before. Not counting all the funerals I have mentioned to her, she knows the score.

I moved my thumb this week, which is a real breakthrough. My first digit to get moving. I can have all the movement in the world in my arm but what use is it without my hand. I have learnt that the same nerve that controls the thumb also controls the forefinger, so I think I will be able to grip objects one day.

Tricia tells me to calm down. 'That would be the case if the nerves were damaged peripherally. With a head injury the whole thing is turned upside down. There is a centre in the brain just for moving the thumb. That's why we can move our thumbs independently of our forefingers.' I sat, stripped to my undies on the bench, looking dejected and confused. She continued, 'So it in no way follows that we should be able to move both the thumb and the forefinger. Anyway your arm is very important for balance, even if your hand isn't functioning.'

The associated reaction in my arm resembles the mad flailings of a symphony conductor as he goes for the final moments of the 1812 Overture. It shakes and lifts, outstretched, as it signals for the cymbals to come in and now to the snare drums.

I see other couples coping with a head-injured man or woman together and wonder what I did wrong. Andie's so loving to Marty and Lydia is equally as loving to Phil. Mopping their brows and fattening them up. I have developed an empathy with Fliss who was in a terrible car accident where she lost her husband and was told her two-and-a-half-year-old son would never walk.

I know that my tragedy in no way compares to hers but what we have in common is neither of us has a partner to share the distress with. We can talk all we want to friends but they don't really have an emotional involvement with us. They can just forget about it when they shut their eyes at night.

19th August

I had to do a walk in the Swedish knee cage yesterday. This may sound horrific, like medieval torture apparatus, but it is simply a splint to help a knee stop hyper-extending. Combined with my drop foot splint, my leg had the appearance of being completely built out of plastic and steel, like the bionic man. Anyway I succeeded in walking my first hundred metres.

Caroline, an outpatient, was here today. I always look forward to seeing her though she only comes in once a month. She's a brash woman who has had a stroke and was in a coma for seven months. She thinks she looks like something out of *Star Trek* but I don't notice. You can tell that she isn't being entirely honest with herself and that sometimes, in the dead of night, she will wake up crying tears for what she once was. 'I used to be a right stunner,' she said. 'I look in the mirror now and don't recognise what I'm seeing.'

Caroline says that she loves being a spastic so she can cause a scene whenever and wherever she likes, which she frequently does. She told a story of how she was in a crowded bar once and shouted out loud, 'I need a shit' to her boy friend. He, incidentally, has left her because he said that she wasn't the dollybird he went out with in the beginning, but a fat cow now. She retorted that she 'was still good in bed though'.

20th August

Lise put me through the first part of my three-monthly COTNAB (Chessington Occupational Therapy Neurological Assessment Battery) test today. I had had it before when I first came on the Unit. I recognised segments of the test but for the most part I hadn't a clue that I'd even seen it before. It's hard to imagine that my memory was ever that poor – my poor memory is just a distant memory.

There were sets of pictures, which I had to put in sequence, a plane taking off or a battery, for some reason, in the distance and getting nearer. There were angles, which I had to arrange from the most acute to obtuse, and dots getting bigger in size from microscopic to an inch in diameter. This first part of the test is entitled Visual Perception and, I suppose, is to let the therapists know if you are safe crossing a busy road, that kind of thing.

21st August

Excitement today as a BBC film crew was here, well Maggie doing the interview and a man whose name I can't remember behind the camera. They want to film my progress throughout the year and then fly me back to Tasmania. I was wary at first but that was because I didn't think I would be strong enough. Now I definitely know I will be fit, so I'm looking forward to it immensely.

Vera, the ward manager, and Ms Young seem to worry an awful lot about my laid back approach to film, book and mortgage contracts. I can see their concern because many head-injury patients seem to have not a care in the world, while I, on the other hand, have been like this all my life. It is convincing them of this fact that is the problem. Vera even asked my mother, 'Do you notice any changes in your son's behaviour?'

My mum, knowing me better than anyone, replied, 'He thinks more of his old mother now.'

The first filming to be done was Lise taking me for occupational therapy. I noticed that she had put eyeliner on. She said she was nervous about filming but on camera she appeared very relaxed. Next came my physio session. Tricia was worried about other physios criticising what she said and took her time over the answers but she spoke perfectly and with authority. I think we made a good team.

24th August

Continuing with the COTNAB test today, this time it's my constructional ability that's under investigation. I felt rushed and made a hash of what I did better at last time, three months ago. It was just building a model out of wooden blocks and it had to be exactly right. Oh well, you can't get everything right.

25th August

I had to put my hand in a black box this morning as part of this COTNAB thingy, to test my sensory motor, in other words touch. I guessed ten assorted items with my eyes closed and my hands being manipulated around them for me.

Then I had to make a coat hanger out of a piece of wire following written instructions. That was the only part of the whole test I was still impaired on. Following the diagrams was easy and I built a model of I don't know what in no time.

27th August

At last. My leg and foot are not as reactive. It didn't quiver and shake and try, like a hammer drill, to make a hole in the floor, as it has done. I walked up the corridor with much better hip control and so the knee followed. Tricia was almost as excited as I was.

Ms Young, my consultant, has come in to see me as I write this journal and told me, 'The tone in your arm is excellent but you shouldn't expect great things from your hand.' It was as though she had built up my hopes and then razed them to the ground just as quickly. She is a cheeky woman who always seems intent on making me blush. In fact I feel like a child before her. She seemed shocked when I suggested that I still wanted to climb or parapente. What else would I do if I couldn't climb? I would be happy just trekking, looking at the mountains, wandering about at their feet. As long as I can still be in the mountains, that's all I ask of fate.

4th September

'A stitch in time saves nine.' 'A bird in the hand is worth two in the bush.' 'A bad workman always blames his tools.' These are some of the proverbs I had to give translations for in OT. All I had to do was say what they really mean but I couldn't; I could only repeat what Lise was saying. I couldn't get my head around them at all. I knew what they meant but I could not find the words to describe them. It was as if I was taking them literally.

In neuro-psychology Fiona read me two stories. One was about a national park and culling a thousand elephants, the other about a band of gypsies who ram-raided shops and robbed bank cash dispensers. They were each four sentences long, but when asked to repeat them back I only retained twenty-five per cent of them whereas unimpaired folk would retain at least fifty per cent. What

I do retain I retain for a long time. In fact, I still remembered the gist of the stories she told me three months ago. You may think that this is contradictory to what I achieved in my COTNAB test, but I apparently have a better memory for words than anything else.

I have been through a range of emotions since being told I haven't to expect anything from my hand. From a furious what-the-fuck-does-she-know-about-my-body to a calm acceptance of events. Whatever happens happens kind of thing. I've been trying extra hard to get my hand moving ever since, trying till I'm blue in the face, literally. But it doesn't want to go.

Gulhan Tas, my Turkish physiotherapist, has been taking me all week. She always has a smile for you, wears spectacles on the end of her nose, is simply gorgeous, and would fit in a thimble, which belies her power. She talks with a strong Turkish accent, a bit like Countess Dracula. She leaves for her next four months in Respiratory in two days and I will be sorry to see her go.

5th September

I moved my forefingers in extension this morning. I can hardly contain myself. It only happened three times but after being told not to expect anything from my hand I think I was even more determined. I'm scared stiff that it will go the same way as my toes and ankle and not move again. I can live without use in my toes and ankle but getting some, even if limited, use of my hand back would be amazing.

Cue Ball's coming into his own now that he has recovered a little. He's still climbing out of bed and ending up on the cold floor but he's also more relaxed in his new surroundings. He's a dreadful flirt with the nurses. He asked Lou to show him her knickers and then, turning his head, grinned a toothless grin, eyes magnified by his jam-jar bottom specs.

7th September

This Monday I've come back to the Unit with a mystery illness. I have swollen glands and a fever, the usual kind of stuff, but what's confusing the doctor is hundreds of blisters covering my whole body. They itch like hell and if you scratch the top of them they burst in little puddles of water.

As I was lying there under the sheet, the nurses buzzing round, putting Cue Ball to bed behind a curtain, all I could hear, as they cleaned him up, was 'Shag me again' and 'Do it to me again!' They tried to repress their laughter, which came spluttering out. I wondered briefly if old women are as rude. I think not somehow.

7 a.m. in the morning I am wrapped in the sheet like a pupa, my face hidden. I am listening to the squeak of the cloth as Helen the domestic wipes down the surfaces, the chink of ice against plastic as she brings in the water jug, and that noise, barely audible, like a 'clip' as she puts down a cup of tea on the Formica. I wait five minutes, until the tea has cooled, and crawl out of my cocoon resembling a leper with boils all over my face and chest.

As I do my diary I am burning up, wanting to tear the skin off my face, my scrotum, my back, my neck. My guess is that it's chicken pox but the doc thinks not. Vera the ward manager, Carol the secretary, all the nurses and all my mates, in fact everyone but the doctor says it's chicken pox. The doctor, by the way, can't give me a diagnosis, though he has given me the usual antibiotics and anti-histamine syrup.

A middle-aged woman called Freda came in this week for respite. She has multiple sclerosis and she's originally from a village near me. She told me a touching story of how she met a fisherman at the wharf one day and fell in love with him. Her parents were not impressed and wanted their daughter to marry a professional man. When the lad went to Saudi Arabia to earn some money to keep her with she met a yachty at the Menai Straits regatta. After a one night stand she became pregnant and, as was the custom in those days, was forced to marry him. Obviously her parents were delighted. A man who owns his own yacht, a professional man, a rich man. From her wheelchair she grinned and told me that she is still seeing the fisherman, who is married now with kids, too. For nearly forty years they have been carrying on a secret love. She says that one day she'll pluck up the courage to leave her husband and spend the rest of her life with her fisherman.

14th September

'I was being strong because I find courage in your strength,' my mother said to me. It was only a month ago when she found out that she had breast cancer, and only last week that she discovered she had to have a mastectomy.

'But I was being strong because I have a good role model in you,' I answered.

She had brought my sister and me up through our teenage years on her own. They weren't easy years and I was forever getting myself into trouble with teachers or police. She underwent numerous operations about that time; her health seemed to fail her right after her divorce from my dad. We then moved into a tiny flat above a hairdressers and I had to share a room with my mum and sleep on a camp bed.

I went to see Bolton Wanderers play Birmingham City on Saturday. We, the wheelies, were all shepherded into a glass box which was pretty high up, and so we had a good view of the game but, cut off from the noise of the crowd, it lacked the electric atmosphere when the Wanderers scored. There were about two dozen of us, each with a minder lined up behind the glass, the paralysed, the legless, the crippled, a jolly crew of Brummy and Wanderers supporters each shouting as their respective teams put a ball in the net. I began to wonder if there would be an outbreak of hooliganism in the box but there was a policeman standing behind us just in case. Anyway we wiped the floor with them, three goals to Birmingham's one.

After the match I was sitting in the inevitable traffic jam when, without warning, I had a fit. I didn't lose consciousness but I did lose the ability to speak. I couldn't tell my stepfather that I was experiencing a seizure and he thought that I was going to be sick, because I was frothing at the mouth. This was a medium-sized fit and it scared me because I had no warning in the form of an aura. Vera says that they can last for two years after a head injury and then normality can reassert itself again. Or the fits can continue for life. I hope and pray the former is the case.

17th September

Simon had a brain tumour, which he had operated on two years ago. As a result of the injuries sustained during the operation he cannot speak and has to be pushed about in his wheelchair. He communicates by pressing a keyboard that synthesises an artificial voice. It's taken me five months to get to know him, mainly because he's an outpatient who only comes in for therapy but also because I was scared of him. I can't tell you what I was scared of. Maybe it's the way he constantly drools and has to have a box of Kleenex on his wheelchair shelf at all times. Or perhaps it's that electronic voice simulator that makes him sound inhuman.

It would be easy to dismiss Simon as a simpleton, but it would be your loss. He has a cracking sense of humour. He keeps asking me how I change the colour of my hair, saying that he would like to go blond. But his wife won't have any of it and says that he's got black hair and it's staying black. I like to wind him up about it and say that he should take control of his own affairs.

His wife, Tracey, who is the mother of his two children, is very beautiful and he must seem intensely ugly to the stranger in the street. She could have any husband she wanted, but has stood by him these two years. It goes to show that it takes more than physical attraction to make a couple, and that family unity is a very strong thing, something that I know precious little about. He may be shocking to look at but, once you talk to him he is intelligent, witty and obviously loving to his family.

All I know is that relationships seem to fall apart in this place with monotonous regularity. Marty's engagement is now on the rocks and he is really cut up about that. You don't hear his filthy old man's laugh echoing down the corridor now, and you certainly don't hear his other more hysterical laugh that sounds like a booming foghorn. Time was when we thought there were two people in his room both laughing at the same TV show.

Kevin is playing footy with Bazza on the parallel bars and he's loving it. He holds himself up on the bars whilst giving a running commentary of the Liverpool squad. 'Fowler to Owen, back to Macmanaman, Berger with a nice pass to Owen who is running the length of the pitch, strikes, and it's in the back of the net.' Bazza, who helps serve our meals, is tapping the sponge ball towards Kevin and he is laughing and swearing as he tries to kick it back. 'I can't fuckin' do it. I'm shit since that bastard put me in 'ere,' he says, speaking of the drunk driver.

Phil walked straight in front of a bus and now staggers around expressionless, speechless. He isn't supposed to go walkabout but when the nurses are busy they can't stop him. Phil has what is called a peg, which is a feeding tube that goes straight into his stomach. He has to push a stand around with him all the time with a bottle of sickly looking liquid in it. I recognise the bottle from my naso-gastric feeding tube days. Anyway, he keeps tampering with the peg and disconnecting the tube and expensive pink fluid runs into the carpet. The built-in alarm on the stand sounds and the nurses come rushing to rectify the problem. That probably happens about twenty times a day.

Lydia, Phil's wife, who was a nurse herself, told me of the five stages to accepting your injury. Denial, anger, bargaining, depression and acceptance. She told me DABDA was how I could remember this. I've had the denial, where I refused to admit I was like other people who used wheelchairs and thought that I would be resuming my round the world climbing trip once this little hiccup was dealt with. The anger has torn me up inside especially when Celia left me. I remember lashing out and telling her that she'd ruined my life. I've done the bargaining bit when I asked the question why didn't I go to Cochimo in Chile instead? That's where my friends were going and where I would have gone if it were not for this round the world trip which led me to the Totem Pole. I've had my moments of depression, but nothing to speak of. I just got bored with being depressed and snapped myself out of it. I don't seem to have a depressive streak in me. And I've calmly accepted my fate from about week six, apart from the denial, which has been a little harder to rub off. These five stages to acceptance can come in any order.

18th September

It is definitely chicken pox that I am suffering. The blisters are getting better but I scratched the tops off most of them before I knew of the scarring. I don't care, I've got more important problems to worry about. Don't ask me how I came about the pox which, incidentally, I had as a child. All I know is that I'm one of those rare cases who are capable of catching it twice.

I wiggled my middle two toes again today. There is a twenty per cent improvement in my memory for stories, word for word, and my concentration has considerably improved. That's the report from Fiona, my neuro-psychologist. My leg seems to have stopped trying to drill holes in the floor but I am now walking like someone from the Ministry of Silly Walks, with the knees very bent. This is in an effort to prevent that old chestnut, the knee flick-back, which is all it takes to start a forceful reaction.

I have been told that I'm going home in three weeks if all's well. I suddenly came over all nervous about life on the outside. I think I'm more institutionalised than I previously thought. I have come to rely on my midweek time here. It gives me a total rest in preparation for the weekend once again. Having all my meals cooked for me, my bed made and fresh sheets put on, my bedroom (or ward) tidied, being bed bathed and showered, having your arse wiped, in Tasmania, and being thoroughly monitored twenty-four hours a day is bound to have some effect after eight months.

This level of pampering is needed at first but there comes a time when you need to stand on your own two feet again. Like a teenager leaving home for the first time you feel a great deal of apprehension as you step out into the cold.

I expected to be in here till the end of the year, although no one actually told me so. The 12th October seems very soon. I promised myself that I would be walking out of these sliding doors when I go and that seems impossible in three weeks. It's just a goal I set myself, that's all.

25th September

After six months, Vera came in to tell me that I haven't to have the injections each morning into my belly. That is one less drug I am dependent on and it feels very liberating. I am up on my feet more now and at less risk from blood clots and thromboses, though I believe that I could have done without them months ago. I guess Ms Young, the consultant neurologist, didn't know just how active I was at the weekend and I wasn't going to let on to her.

Moving into the new house was blissful. The boys had built me a ramp to get into the kitchen, shake-'n'-vac-ed the carpets, hung pictures, got a fire going in the hearth and generally made it homely. It is much smaller than the old house, has cat shit in the back yard and doesn't have the views of Yr Wyddfa and Clogwyn Du'r Arddu that I'm used to, but it is mine.

30th September

'Nervous centres represent movements, not muscles. From lesions of motor centres there is not paralysis of muscles but loss of movements.'

Hughlings/Jackson, 1958

I have been hassling Vera and Tricia for reading matter on the brain, anything to do with neurology really. The two of them have had to put up with my constant questions and incessant enthusing for six months now. On my desk there is a pile of books referring to brains which is two feet high and growing.

I cooked a Taiwanese dish yesterday. Tofu with red pepper and fresh coriander. I think I'm coming on in the kitchen. I asked Lise to get me the tools I will need to aid cooking in my new home: electric tin-opener, spike board, left-handed scissors, brush for washing dishes that sticks onto the side of the sink, extraordinarily sticky cloth for opening jars, knife with the handle at a right angle to the blade to ease grip, the list goes on.

Last night the Cue Ball was truly animated and his voice had a clarity that I'd never heard before. He was pointing at Marty, calling him rude, and laughing like a maniac, his cue ball head and oversized eyes behind his specs and single tooth adding to the effect. It was good to see. We all joined in their infectious laughter and pretty soon we were doubled over ourselves. There was Joy, Jill and Hilary of the night nurses, Hilda, Dawn, Karen and Marty of the patients.

Hilda was struck down with the Gillam/Beri virus, which affected her spine and left her paralysed for a short time. She's back up on her feet now though, another example of the hope there is in here. Dawn is a young girl, perhaps a teenager who wiped a car out. She has all her mental faculties about her but shuffles her feet, that's all. And Karen is suffering from multiple sclerosis for which there is no known cure.

I have been practising walking up stairs all this week. I can lift my knee but not without my lower leg rising also in a kind of goose step. This is because my hamstring is still refusing to function unless I surprise it. Then it works. But how do you surprise a muscle? By the time you've thought about surprising it, it is a surprise no longer. So I must not think about the hamstring, effectively ignoring it and then, suddenly, take action. Then it bends back as easy as pie. Until I can achieve being able to will my knee to bend I am stuck with having to trail my right leg up each step.

1st October

The day of the Case Conference

I felt like a schoolboy going into the headmaster's office as I passed through that door with my short pants on (I had just come out of my physio session). It is strategically positioned at the end of a long corridor so you see it there for what feels like miles as you are wheeled down. I felt as though I had to tell them everything. There were, perhaps, ten 'grown-ups' circled around a large table asking me questions like 'Who empties your commode for you?' and 'Who do you have to shop for you?' Most of them I knew pretty well. There was Lise and Tricia, Vera and Mark, Ann the social worker and Dr Shakespeare, but now they assumed a level of 'grown-upness' that was terrifying. I went red in the face and started to sweat. I tried to get a smile out of Tricia but she could not allow herself, in front of the others, the familiarity which is born out of spending an hour every day with me.

Coming clean about how many times I really climbed the stairs was a hard task, but I knew I had to do it if I was going to avoid having a lift put in. The lift would have been a good joke but hardly worth the ten-grand council grant. I told them that I didn't need anyone to empty the commode for me because I didn't use it. And I told them that I did my own shopping. I was laughing nervously. They just looked at me as if to say, 'You'll be sorry when you come crashing down those stairs.' I felt stupid and it wasn't them that made me feel that way.

They decided to come and witness for themselves 'the great event' of me climbing the stairs and also getting in and out of a bath. When I told my therapists I could do this they looked aghast. A hemiplegic at this stage of recovery should not be able to have a bath without complex equipment but, being a climber, I have certain strengths that other folk don't have, namely good balance and the ability to push up with one arm.

6th October

The date for my release has been put back to the 15th. That's what they call it, a 'release', as if it were prison or something. I guess you can draw parallels with being inside but that wouldn't be helpful. I've been sentenced to six months' love and attention. It doesn't seem that way to some patients though. They can't wait to get out, even though their bodies patently aren't well. They grow bored, as prisoners do, with the monotonous regularity of traipsing down to the dining area for three lousy meals a day. Being confined, losing your freedom, having to sign an 'out book' whenever you want to go to the shop, not having an ounce of privacy, sleeping as I have done for the last eight months on wards, the small quadrant all fenced in and locked up, but perhaps the most enduring image of prison life are the nurses' paces up and down the dark corridor, just like a warder's.

The fear of institutionalisation is ever present and, indeed, I felt more than a grain of this when they told me I was free to go on 12th October. I became nervous and irritated and for some time I didn't know why. Then it became clear, I was becoming institutionalised and the release date was sooner than I expected. So I told myself that I'd better make the break before becoming totally so – or rather they told me. The Rehab Unit's staff seem to know just about everything about anything relating to what's best for you. You don't see it at first; it only becomes apparent in retrospect.

I went to a fine party at the weekend to help warm a friend's new house. When I got home, about 3 a.m., and put the grill on because I had the munchies, I stumbled over the blasted wheelchair and fell on the concrete floor. I went over like a felled tree and my head missed the radiator by inches. When I fall, my body always topples to my right and my elbow, not my hand, automatically comes out to protect me thus transmitting the forcible blow to my already damaged shoulder. I lay there for about twenty minutes clutching at my paining joints, somewhat shocked, before I clambered up into my chair and took myself off to bed.

Back in the Unit I told Tricia that I'd gone off the kerb in my wheelchair, because I was terrified that they were going to delay my release date. This then made me feel overwhelmingly childish. I'm a grown man. Why do I feel the need to tell trivial lies? But it wasn't trivial to me. My future was in balance. Me on one scale and a giant organisation on the other. However many hospital dinners I ate I couldn't tip the balance in my favour. I didn't know what powers the National Health Service had to keep me inside. Was I becoming paranoid? I mean really. The very thought of it was absurd.

7th October

Stephen is a patient who does three days a week here and is pencil thin, as are many of the folk in rehab, those who aren't grossly overweight that is. They lose weight from the injuries they have sustained. His choice of vocabulary isn't always brilliant, so he tells me, and then proceeds to use words like 'anathema' and 'mammon' all the time. The only problem with his words is that they are perhaps too long and used in the wrong context. But he might have always been like this. His right side feels heavy but you wouldn't know there was anything wrong with him. He would just be a 'strange fish' on the outside. He's a publican who was in a car accident, luckily on his own, near Abergele.

I'm really excited about my new life on the outside. Not only am I leaving hospital and leaving my home of three years but I've bought a new house and my relationship with Celia has ended. I've also had to quit climbing, which is a major life-changing event in itself. I've been climbing for fifteen years and now I've been put in a wheelchair. Now some may ask, what's exciting about that? Downright bad luck I say. But that would be missing the opportunity to learn from pain. I've learnt about inner strengths I was never aware of until fate put me in this situation. Some people would say that I lived for my climbing but I would say that I lived through my climbing. Surviving it obviously, but growing through it also. I'm confident things are going to work out OK, you have to keep a positive attitude. There's always something to focus on and you can take comfort, if you wish, in the knowledge that there is always someone worse off than yourself. That's not hard in here where there are several patients worse off than me. (The Cue Ball was stuffing his face with a plate of food yesterday and there wasn't even a plate in front of him.)

13th October

This is my last week at the Unit. My final full day, in fact I'm leaving tomorrow. In some ways I'll be sad to leave, it has become such a big part of my life.

In my semi-conscious state I can hear Margaret and Helen, the stewardesses, chatting about nothing in particular outside the French windows while they have their first fag break of the day. They're as regular as clockwork. My life is as regular as clockwork these last six months. I lazily rouse myself out of bed, it's 8.30, turn my computer on, open the curtains to look at the weather from the safety of my double-glazed shield, wheel myself into the bathroom to douse my hair with cold water, clean my teeth, get dressed, go and make myself coffee in the OT kitchen. I then work on my computer for two hours, take my anti-convulsants which I should take the moment I get up but they make me too drowsy to work, and then it's time for lunch. Sometimes therapy interrupts my routine which can be a good thing if I've nothing to say and I'm staring at a blank screen but if I'm busy writing I get hacked off because I lose my train of thought.

Tricia allowed me to walk with a stick today. It felt so liberating after being in that chair for eight months. I walked for seventy metres from the physio gym across the dining room, past the office and down the corridors, passing all the wards. I think I'll walk to Pete's Eats Cafe tomorrow, imagine what the guys' faces will be like when I just walk in with only my stick for balance. Then I will go to the counter and casually order a brew, I can't carry full cups yet so I will have to get Sara to fetch it to the table. Then I'll sit down with my mates and sup it.

There was a veritable feeding time at the zoo at dinner tonight. There was Cue Ball eating an invisible plateful of food again and there was Marty complaining, 'I'm not eating this crap.' There was a tiny sparrow of a woman who I'd never seen before lying in her bed which was wheeled into the day room by the nurses. She cried like a sparrow chick. 'Cheep. Cheep. Cheep.' And then there was Kevin telling the poor woman to 'Shut up, will you.' There was Cue Ball shouting 'Everton, Everton,' even though he's a Preston North End supporter and Phil was stroking the sparrow woman's hand lovingly, trying to calm her.

14th October

'The sights you see when you haven't got a gun,' joked Brenda the nurse fresh back from her holiday in Hawaii. She was behind the curtain with other nurses, Burt and Jill, and referring to the naked body of Rodney who lay, beetle-like on his back, with limbs waving in the air. That's the scene I woke up to this morning.

But I was content in the knowledge that it was my final day. No more nights in that hospital bed, no more Rodney rattling his cot sides in the dead of night, no more Kevin shouting in his disinhibited manner in the early morning, no more Marty screaming, 'Get off my leg! Get off my arm!' because of his hypersensitivity. No more nurses in white uniforms, no more ward sister in her blue uniform, no more sitting at this very desk, at this very laptop, tapping away. No more overcooked dinners and no more evenings spent in front of the TV watching whatever trash is on the screen because nobody can be arsed to change the channel. No more occupational therapy, no more neuro-psychology, and no more physio with Tricia. That I'm not too pleased about. No more sitting out in the quadrant with a tab of an evening in shirt-sleeves and no more reclining out there in the sunshine. No more plastic cups of tea brought round by Pat, Helen, Liz or Margaret. No more Joy, Jill, Margy, Pat, Sue, Vera, the two Marks, Jenny, Brenda, Bert, Carol, Pauline, Julie, the two Christines, Hilary, Jean, Shirley, Irene, Mo, Lou, Bert, Ev.

19th October

Fontainebleau

I left rehab on the Wednesday and took off, by way of celebration, to Fontainebleau on Thursday. My first trip for nine months. Memories of the nightmare repatriation flight came back to me, as I was crammed in the back of a transit with six other men, between two wheel arches. It was beautiful in the forest, although I did have a twinge of enviousness as I watched all my mates exercising on the boulders. Fontainebleau is renowned for being the best bouldering area in the world and I really did enjoy my bouldering before the accident. Climbing in its simplest form, just you and the rock. No ropes or hardware, no harnesses or slings, no helmets getting in the way. Fortunately, it rained for two of the four days we were there which meant that I had playmates to do what I wanted to do with, that is sit in pavement cafes, sipping expressos and watching the world going by.

1st November

After over ten months without sex I started to seriously doubt whether I could get it up, and if I could get it up, would my crippled body perform? I mean not only had I not done it for ten months but I had a serious head injury to contend with as well. Last night it happened over a couple of bottles of wine and it has rejuvenated me and made me feel normal again. I knew that I wouldn't be able to get in to all the positions that I used to but there is something inherently submissive and humbling about lying on your back and being made love to. We stayed in all evening when all around were partying and the children were knocking on the door and trick-or-treating. That's just one more healing process complete.

10th November

Since coming out of the Rehab my walking has been improving at an exponential rate. I am toddling a full half mile now which, after nine months, I think, means I've picked this walking business up faster than a baby. That is encouraging because it is effectively what I am doing, learning to walk from scratch. I have progressed from lying on my back in my cot, legs and arms waving in the air, to crawling and scraping around on the floor, to toddling. Apparently the conscious brain tries to put a padlock on the brain stem and hinder your walking, so it becomes more difficult to learn to walk again the older and more set in your ways you've become.

I definitely felt like a baby, walking on Porth Oer, which is a beach on the Lleyn Peninsula, seeing things with new eyes. The colour of the mud was a vibrant orange, the sand had all shades of grey in it, and whistled too, and the sea was a truly beautiful shade of green. It seemed as though I were wandering inside a Benedict Bevan Pritchard painting under crazy apocalyptic skies on the shore of an ocean reaching out to me and licking my feet. After a quarter of a mile I turned at a huge white tooth sticking out of the sand and returned slowly to the car.

13th November

My old friend Penny Croxford described my predicament thus: 'Neural networks are like footpaths and the more frequently they're used the better condition they're in. If they are left to fall into dereliction they become overgrown and more difficult to walk down. So it's in your interest to keep trying, using that footpath.' Penny's my physiotherapist at Bangor whom I received treatment from for a whole month with Stormont Murray before going to Clatterbridge. After nine months I've found my conviction for doing the arm exercises ebbing, in fact I haven't done any for an entire month.

Barbara is her superior; she didn't recognise me when I walked in, so used was she to seeing me in a wheelchair. We had an assessment today to see what my needs were. More hand and arm movement seems to be the order of the day and more balance in walking. My arm will work, of sorts, for five or so moves and then gets tired and gives up.

I knocked on the workshop door of Joy Hughes, the OT. Upon entering I was astounded to see all the splints and casts covering a whole wall. At a glance there appeared to be racks and masks and iron maidens and other articles of anguish. With all the sprung splints and gloves and finger casts it looked like Madame Whiplash's torture chamber. And across the opposite wall were the machines that did God only knows what, machines with pulleys and levers and switches, handles that turn rollers, keys that turn in locks, Velcro items that stick to other Velcro items, cones, putty of all colours in pots, abacuses and rubber equipment. I would be visiting this place twice a week from now on.

17th November

David Rosenbaum in his book *Human Motor Control* suggests how a patient might regain control of a limb by seeing an image of the limb with greater mobility than it actually has. He describes an experiment (Rock and Harris, 1967) where subjects were told that if they put their hand in a box they would be able to see it moving through a window. Unbeknown to the subjects, they were looking at the experimenter's hand and as long as it moved in synchronicity with the subjects' they couldn't tell the difference. So it makes sense that giving the illusion of a limb moving can provide the incentive for me to attempt to move the limb on my own.

I now have textbooks and papers on neuro-psychology, neuro-physiology, neuro-biology, basic neurology, motor control, learning and memory. Then there are lay books such as *How the Mind Works*, *No Ghost in the Machine*, *Phantoms in the Brain* and *Emotional Intelligence*. I find that I am in a much better position to get a handle on my predicament if I can begin to understand it. The human brain is the most complicated of organs with over a hundred billion cells and more possible connections than there are atoms in the whole universe, so no one can truly understand it. But you can have a pretty good go.

24th November

I visited Clatterbridge again today to be discharged by my final therapist, Lise. Fiona, Tricia and Siobhan discharged me when I left the Unit but Lise had to see how I was faring at home. I walked down a grass banking with Dave Green pushing my chair behind me. The chair, incidentally, hasn't been used for a month and I was taking it back today. I felt like I was marching at the front of a procession with a cheesey grin on my face and all the nurses and therapists looking on in a row from behind the glass door. Sitting in the day room watching TV were a few new faces. Kevin remembered my name and where I came from but couldn't remember what football team I support. It was good to see him. I know which pub he gets taken to by his father. I will go and drink a pint with him one day.

Marty didn't know who I was and it was as difficult as ever to engage him in conversation, as he talks at you rather than with you. His twisted wrist and feet look better after the corrective surgery. It is distressing not to be recognised by somebody who you have seen every day for two months. 'My name's Paul,' I said, but he just looked at me and replied, 'Have you just been home for the weekend?' attempting to mask his non-recognition. He had no idea that he hadn't seen me for six weeks. He'll get better though.

Cue Ball was out for the count, catching flies, with the back of his cue ball head resting on a pillow. Phil had his head on the table and seemed to be frustrated with something, agitated. I don't know if he recognised me but when I enquired how he was, he simply replied, 'I'm fucked.' There were a few less angelfish in the tank. Either they just keep dying or the monster plec keeps devouring them. It was good to see Jenny and Pauline and Mark and Vera and Lise, too.

27th November

It was the Lentil and Merlin who drove me up to Liverpool's Fazakerley Hospital for a MRI (Magnetic Resonance Imaging) scan. I was shown to a cubicle and had to change into a gown that tied up the back, so I needed helping. I walked to the scanner barefoot, which is always painful because my toes clench onto the floor so tightly and unavoidably. Being led into a green room I saw a gargantuan machine, like an industrial tumble-dryer. My ears were plugged and head locked in place and I was slid into the tumbler.

The assistant cleared off behind a lead-lined glass screen so as not to get too many radioactive rays. There was a lot of clicking and whirring and, in the background, the sound of a jet plane taking off. Then the voice of an air stewardess was asking me if I was OK and comfortable enough over an intercom. Suddenly I began to wiggle my toes and in the excitement of it all forgot to keep my head perfectly still. The radiologist had to repeat the photographs four times before she was happy with the result.

We then headed to the Salvador Dali exhibition at the Tate Gallery in Albert Dock, a place I am getting to know rather well. After having my brain dealt with in the scanner I was now having it bent by the Dali paintings of dripping clocks and telephones on crutches.

1st December

I have put ads in the cafe and shops and outdoor centres around here, 'CLIMBING GEAR FOR SALE'. Two pairs of ice axes, two pairs of crampons, literally hundreds of nuts, cams and karabiners, ten pairs of rock shoes and four pairs of plastic mountaineering boots, stoves, helmets, ropes, skis, sleeping bags, bivvi bags and assorted clothing. Literally thousands of pounds worth of kit.

I had no idea how much it would hurt to get rid of my equipment until the first guy showed his face at the door. It felt as though I was selling fifteen years of existence down the river. I was choking up as he was rummaging through my life, trying on my boots and checking my helmet for fit. I had to turn away and hide my tears when he asked me how much. With each piece of cloth or metal came another memory; those boots I wore climbing that gully on Meru, in the Garhwal Himalaya, and that rope created a thread between Celia and me as we moved together on L'Aleta de Tiburon, the Shark's Fin in Paine, Chilean Patagonia. And there on the window sill was the blood-soaked windproof which they had to cut off me when I was in pre-op. Don't ask me how it found its way back here. It was like some grisly holiday souvenir that was following me to the ends of the earth.

10th December

I threw all my notes on mountains away about three months ago. I didn't know what I was doing. All I knew was that I didn't want all this stuff cluttering up my life any more. I had boxes of information that only I have and now it's gone into the shredder – topos, diagrams, lists, photos, maps and drawings all on the garbage heap. When someone came around the other day to use my library, my mine of information, I guiltily told her, 'Look, I threw it away in a rage.' At least I didn't incinerate my slides, of which I have thousands. I must have been wearing some sort of self-preservation helmet.

15th December

Wirral Neuro Rehabilitation Unit Christmas party.
I caught the train for the first time since my injury and on my own, too. This may not sound like much but I was frightfully intimidated. Scared that I wouldn't be able to get onto the trains

or that I would miss my connections, and worried, too, that I wouldn't be able to get off in time at the relevant station. As it turned out it was a breeze and I shouldn't have troubled my head about it at all. I guess your self-confidence and self-esteem take a crippling blow when you've been through what I have. But I am a pretty stoic chap and I'm now regaining much of what I may have lost.

Cathy and Angel met me at the station and took me to the Unit's Christmas party. All the loons were there and a fair few patients as well. Dave's had his knees broken so he didn't look like his legs were on display any more. He's overjoyed about that, you can see it in his eyes. After twenty years of waiting he has good reason to be. His feet are next. Marty recognised me so his cognition is improving and, although Phil still doesn't remember me, he is very pleasant and always acknowledges me. Kevin has left, an important event seeing that he has been there nearly two years. He was awaiting a bathroom extension being built and when that was finished he was out of there. He is still making improvement, albeit by very small increments and perhaps he will get better more quickly, as I have done, once he's home.

Cue Ball was still there, mouth agape, his bald head tilted right back. Jean has sadly gone into an old folks' home, even though she's not that old. It's just that her husband can't, or doesn't want to, look after her. I remember her family discussing what to do with her. Her daughter wasn't too happy with the arrangement, her son was accepting of it and her husband, who looked like a Nepali with a skull cap, was all for it.

The very first thing I did when I walked into the day room was check out the fishtank which was down to two angelfish and the ever-growing plec, which may or may not have eaten the others. Carol the secretary was busy serving tumblers of wine through the hatch while, on their second bottle of vodka, some nurses, the usual suspects, were trying to recreate the summer barbecue (and succeeding). I won a bottle of brandy on the tombola, which was the only prize suitable for me amidst a sea of pink knitted toilet roll covers and baskets of soap. Cathy and I spent most of the time round the 'smokers' corner' having a crack with Joy, Mark, Lou, Jean, Dee and Shirley.

But the party was a little sad because I knew that that was it. I couldn't go on returning to Clatterbridge, so I was saying my farewells to the place. However much grief the actual building gave me I have very fond memories of the staff and patients there. They had become like family to me but when I walked into that day room my head filled with ghosts, so I have to divorce myself from it totally.

1st January, 1999

My New Year's resolution is simply to get down to some work again. I've been, how shall we say, 'on one' ever since I left Clatterbridge, celebrating, partying as if I'd just come out of the nick which is effectively where I'd been for nine months. OK, so I was allowed home at weekends but so are some prisoners; I still had to sign an 'out book' whenever I wanted to go to the canteen. Obviously there is a good reason for this as you couldn't have brain-damaged patients running amok all over the place. Clatterbridge was very conducive to writing; it was either watch the telly or sit at my computer and write, so there was really no choice. But my workrate has plummeted in the past ten weeks since leaving the Unit, there are so many diversions and distractions.

My friends have been talking, worriedly, about my consumption of alcohol and how that will mix with my anti-convulsants. I appreciate their concern but I have a good idea of what my limits are and the fact that I have lived through it and am back to writing now must surely count for something. It just felt like a thing I had to do, a blow out, and everyone's entitled to a blow out once in a while, especially if you've been locked up for ten months. I'm over it now.

V. S. Ramachandran writes in *Phantoms in the Brain*: 'The right hemisphere [of the brain] is a left-wing revolutionary that generates paradigm shifts, whereas the left hemisphere is a die-hard conservative that clings to the status quo.' I have left hemisphere damage, which supposedly indicates that I cling less to the status quo and generate more paradigm shifts. I'll let you know when that happens.

3rd January

George Smith was 'commissioned' to make a virtual reality mirror box for me and it arrived today. It is a curious thing that attempts to trick the brain into thinking that one has two functioning hands. Placing a mirror vertically inside a cardboard box with the lid removed is all that it takes. The box then has two holes cut in the front through which I was to place my limp right hand and my strong left hand. The reflective side of the mirror is placed so that it faces my left hand and my right hand is hidden behind the mirror if I position my head properly.

The effect is that I see my actual left hand and the reflected image of it representing my right hand. If I were to try moving both hands in synchronicity, would I be able to hoodwink my brain and get my right hand to function again? It is an experiment that I read about in one of my neurology textbooks but in that case it was used for patients with phantom limbs and chronic phantom limb pain. I thought there was a small chance that it could be of some use in hemiplegia, though I couldn't find it documented anywhere. All I can report is that it didn't happen instantly but I expect it to take a few weeks, if it happens at all.

14th January

It is said that Shostakovich had a piece of shrapnel lodged in his brain by a shell explosion in the First World War and if he tilted his head to the right he began hearing incredible symphonies. The shard of metal shifted imperceptibly and stimulated an area of his brain that is geared to creating music. Another patient, at sixty-five, had a stroke and began to appreciate poetry for the first time in his life. Why can't I be like one of these patients whose lives are enhanced by their head injury instead of being beaten and battered? Sometimes I wake up and cannot get out of bed because I am so stiff.

Getting the bus from the station to Wirral Neuro, I suddenly became embarrassed. Maybe I'm hassling them too much. Maybe they don't want me hanging round all the time. There comes a time when you have to break free of these units, however long you've been there. There is the danger of clinging on to the nurses' apron strings when you are let out into the big open yonder. But I was only there to see my medical records and that is my right since the 1992 Medical Records Act.

Jill Chappel is now the head honcho of the physiotherapists. She totally surprised me when she said that we had mutual friends. We shared three friends, two of whom I knew very well. Did she know of me before my accident? I didn't ask her. For eight months she had kept a big secret from me. 'Patient confidentiality,' she answered simply.

In the office of the chief of medical records, Alison Whittlestone, I pored over my notes:

'No evidence of osteomyelitis' . . . 'The right frontal bone extending inferiorly to the floor of the right anterior cranial fossa (superior orbital roof)' . . . 'Frequent delta/theta appear maximal over left temporal region with maximal amplitudes occipitally.'

I had no idea what they were on about but I resolved to find out with the aid of my textbooks. The CT scans of my head from

173

Tasmania looked shocking. There was the thin skin of skull and the grey matter but then, there was a white fuzzy patch virtually covering the whole of the left hemisphere of my brain. This was the site of the impact of the rock and the contusion. I stared at it until I felt nauseous. I had numerous pages photocopied, thanked Ms Whittlestone, and left the office.

9

RETURN TO THE TOTE

People are greater than the arrangements of the world and more powerful than their psychological constituents. Will is all and if we can only realise this, a true transcendence or rising above the rules of the world is possible. In the face of total and moral relativity, the self is immanent, freedom to act is absolute.

Stanley Cohen and Laurie Taylor
Escape Attempts

Finding my air ticket lying on the doormat I was suddenly hit with the reality of my situation. I was going back, flying back to Tasmania, and on my own. If taking the train was new and intimidating, so would be negotiating airports and boarding aeroplanes. I had no idea how I would cope. But I just had to take the bull by the horns and go for it. Then there were the Tasmania Police Force who rescued me, the nurses, the therapists and surgeons to meet up with. I didn't know how I would feel about that; probably highly emotional.

But looming over all of this was the beast itself to confront. That was the real reason why I was going back to Tasmania. That was the essence of why I was flying halfway round the world. It was a pilgrimage and I could not relax until I had gone back to the place, seen the Totem Pole and, more than this, seen the scar that had been left by the rock when it parted company with the face to which it had been attached for a million years or more.

A recurring nightmare began plaguing me that the Totem Pole had turned into a giant sea snake or serpent, or maybe it was a dragon. It had taken on a live scaly appearance and it reared out of the sea in front of me. Its head was level with me as I stood at the rappel point, looking straight into its eyes, its mouth. I could see its fangs, could smell its warm sickly breath, it was so close. At that point I'm not scared as such but then it begins to grow and grow until, like the proverbial beanstalk, it seems to reach the sky. That's when I wake up sweating. I can interpret this dream; firstly, it is the one thing that has changed my life irrevocably and secondly, because I was writing a book about it I haven't had a chance to forget it for one moment. Thirdly, I was imminently returning to the scene of my accident and, not only that, but it would be exactly a year to the day that I would see it again. So it's hardly surprising that I should have such fevered dreams.

The taxi came at 8 a.m. on a drizzly day. The driver, who instantly struck up conversation, fascinated me. He told me he was struggling as an artist and that this job was only a way of making ends meet. He was skinny, middle-aged, had big grey side-burns that held on his mass of curly hair, also grey. During the hour and a half drive to the airport we never shut up and the areas we covered ranged wide.

He told me, when he was a boy he used to go out to Ynys Enlli, an island off the west tip of Gwynedd, for the family summer holiday. One afternoon whilst exploring he came across a nest of snakes and, although scared at first, felt impelled to put his hand into it. He received eight bites and became very ill. 'My parents thought they'd spawned a mad child,' he told me, 'but afterwards I felt strangely uplifted, like I could do anything, tackle anything. I felt invincible.' He said he'd been reading up about the therapeutic properties of snake venom and told me that that is why the British Medical Association have two snakes writhing together as their symbol. This story grabbed my imagination but all too soon we were at Manchester Airport.

No longer could I just sling a rucsac on my back and set off around the world. I had had to buy a plastic suitcase that wheeled along. I felt extremely self-conscious rolling that thing through the airport with all the other business people. But I still managed to look different with my ungainly gait, my leg being thrown out to the right with every step. Occasionally I would stumble, almost fall, forcing passers by to attempt a catch. They would stagger this way and that like a goal keeper in a soccer match who doesn't know where the shot is going to come from, arms out wide. But I never fell. I even took to playing this game where I almost collapsed into the arms of people I knew I could get a reaction out of. An amusing way of meeting folk.

Because of my disability I had innocently assumed that the BBC would have forked out for a first-class ticket and have things laid on a plate for me, but that wasn't to be. I was left to fight my way onto the airliner with 300 other people. At first this really pissed me off but then I thought of it as occupational therapy. I didn't actually want different treatment to everyone else. I desperately wanted to be the same, even if that meant being the last one on and finding all the overhead lockers full. Anger and frustration gripped me in the beginning but towards the end of the flight I mellowed out and learned to relax.

In the departure lounge at Melbourne I was met by the whole film crew, seven in all, who had flown in from the States. The safety team of Mark Diggins, Dave Cuthbertson and John Whittle I know well, as I do the assistant producer, Brian Hall. The producers, Meg Wicks and Richard Else, and the cameraman, Keith Partridge, I have only met through this film. The scale of the operation hadn't really hit me until this moment; we would be ten when we met up with the climbers, Steve Monks and Enga Lokey. It was very apt that they were climbing the Totem Pole for the film because they were the last people Celia and I met before the accident.

I started to panic. What if I couldn't give insightful and interesting answers when interviewed? I often couldn't when I was nervous or put on the spot. I kept my doubts about it all well buried.

Richard and Meg are very professional, and have the knack of leading you on to interesting answers.

During the Melbourne to Hobart flight I sat next to Dan, a Vietnam War veteran from Paradise. Paradise, it turns out, is in Northern California. We got chatting and, after telling him why I was returning to Tasmania, the subject soon turned to near-death experiences. He told me of the time he was in the field and surrounded by Viet Cong guerrillas. It was late at night, he and a friend were keeping watch. They had strung out lines all around the camp and to these had attached tin cans to warn them if the 'commies' were trying to creep up on them. 'A gust of wind must have blown,' he told me, 'the cans rattled and this dude panicked.' Dan became strangely animated. 'He started shooting this Bren gun.' Dan was transported back in time right there. 'Rat tat tat tat tat.' It was as if he was the one firing the machine gun. 'That guy would have cut me in half if some invisible force hadn't pushed me to the ground just in time. To this day I do not know why I hit the deck that night.'

Enga and Steve were there to meet us at Hobart 'International' Airport in wild weather. It was the term 'international' that I found comical for a collection of sheds on a desolate runway. They weren't prepared for how I just sauntered down the steps off the aircraft and across the landing strip. The last time the two of them had seen me I was on my back with no movement or feeling in my right limbs, and only up to the odd grunt.

The last time I saw this patch of tarmac was from a stretcher, horizontal and melancholy, but content to be on my way home. It had started. The flood of memories. I felt like I was on the downstream side of a bursting dam, unable to hold the weight of memories that was cached behind it. I was happy to see Steve and Enga, though it didn't feel like one year since we had last met. It seemed like a lifetime ago since they had come to visit me in the hospital. We drove past familiar landmarks, Seven Mile Beach, the twin causeways out to Sorell and the wine glass stem of Eagle Hawk Neck. When Port Arthur was a penal settlement the guards used to have mad dogs strung out between the two beaches, about a hundred yards apart, to deter escapers.

I allowed my mind to wander. I started to think about all the deaths, over the years, between the shores of this small island. Long before the term 'ethnic cleansing' was invented it took place here. There are no full-blooded aboriginals left to tell the long history of Van Dieman's Land, as it was previously known, just a handful of caves and tools, deep in the bush, to remind us that they once existed. And then there is Port Arthur itself with its Island of the Dead, home to 1700 convict graves. Once murderers and thieves would be sent there but now you pay twenty-five dollars to visit 'the Site'. I thought this ironic. In the ruins of the Broad Arrow cafe I even saw tourists photographing the bullet holes where Bryant let off. There are a lot of ghosts in Tassie.

We arrived at the Fox and Hounds in the dark. All done out like a Tudor mansion, you can visit 'Ye Olde Bottle Shoppe', which is drive through, and drink in the Robert Peel Bar. The hotel was in the grips of a power cut and candle flames danced and flickered in the squinting light. Waitresses like phantoms glided here and there in the semi-lit restaurant. We heard from the manager that the wind had ripped the roof off the house. 'Good timing for a film,' laughed Richard.

I awoke early, unable to lie in, to a morning as still as a moment, the Tasmania I remembered. I opened the back door of the 'cottage' and, bleary-eyed, surveyed the scene. Exotic birds were bleeping and whistling and making sounds that one would think only synthesisers capable of. The sun came up over the gum trees, which looked like giant broccoli spears with the bark hanging off them, like rags off a tramp. The inlet was so smooth and reflective that I felt as if I could take a step onto it and walk about on its salty water.

Although it was only twenty-one years old, the hotel seemed ancient, like one you would expect to find in the Highlands of Scotland. The obligatory coach party from Yorkshire, or in this case Melbourne, turned up for breakfast, all slacks and purple rinses.

We joined them, suffering from jet lag, in a scrum for the buffet. Then I made my way outside again.

The pulse of a helicopter, which was no stranger to me, only just perceptible to begin with, got louder and louder until it ruptured the tranquil atmosphere of the morning. A floatplane had to be moved and the machine landed by the loch-side. I was stunned to see that the name of the company was Helicopter Resources, the same people who had rescued me, though this was a different pilot and another machine. I was told that I was having a rest day after my arduous flight, while the others rigged the stack for filming. In the first foray were Steve and Enga who knew Cape Hauy very well. Hopefully they could find a spot, flat and clear of trees, to put the helicopter down.

After twenty minutes Bill the pilot returned with a worried look on his face.

'There's one landing place on the whole bloody peninsula and even that's crook. I just can't put her down there. I'll have to keep the rotor going and just sit the skis down on the rocks. Think you can handle that?'

Was he questioning me? I hadn't a clue whether I could handle escaping from a hovering helicopter. The nearest I'd come to that since my injury was getting out of the passenger door of a stationary Fiat Panda.

I mooched around for the day quite glad to have time to meditate on my position. I was sitting reading on the front doorstep when a pickup pulled up on the roadside in front of the cottage and out jumped a burly guy with tattoos on his arms. He pulled a spade from the back of the truck and with one scrape scooped up a wallaby corpse. There's a huge number of dead animals on the road in Tassie, echidnas, pademelons, poteroos and the famous Tassie devil. I thought what more satisfying job could one have than scraping road kill up for the council! That evening I realised just how film crews are forced to survive on BBC expense accounts.

Sleep wouldn't take me that whole long night, even though I

tried to anaesthetise myself with wine, knock myself out with brandy. In my mind I was running over the scene of the accident again and again, swinging in that long arc on the end of the rope and then . . . nothing. Celia's voice shouting to me, blood in the sea, being hauled up on the end of a cord eight millimetres thin, the struggling to get onto the ledge, fighting a losing battle to stay awake whilst the blood pooled on the shelf. I could still hear Neale's words, 'You'll be all right, cobber,' as he tried to comfort me. All these things, it seemed, only happened yesterday.

I was terrified of flying in the helicopter which in my imagination now represented a sinister menace. I had been only barely conscious the other three times I had flown in one, for they were all rescue operations. For the Gogarth incident and the Creagh Meghaidh accident I was in an extremely traumatised state and during my rescue from the Totem Pole I remember the incessant noise of the helicopter like some bad dream. So I associated that damn machine with suffering and pain and nightmares. Even though it had saved my life on three occasions and I felt eternally indebted to the pilots and flight crew, I was positively frightened of getting into one. And how I would perform dismounting from a hovering helicopter I could only guess.

Sleep overcame me just as dawn was breaking and the next thing a larger than life John Whittle was calling to me, 'It's blowing some but I think we'll fly.' Poet, philosopher and pianist, John Whittle has been described as the Leonard Cohen of British rock. As much at home playing classical or jazz, Bach or Gershwin, his stocky frame and stumpy fingers belie his charming nature. He has swept back white hair and a musical voice which can disarm even the hardest soul.

When the helicopter came in to land I realised why everyone was wearing long trousers. The sand blew up under the rotors and stung my legs something rotten. We waited for the rotor blades to stop before I was bundled in between Keith and Brian. Enga was up front next to Bill, the pilot. The engines started to roar and we lifted slowly out of the trees before accelerating over the water. Each time we dropped, ten feet or more, my heart would jump into my mouth and my testicles would find their way into my stomach.

The first feature I recognised amidst the green blanket of gum trees was the crescent moon of white sand that is Fortescue Bay. We carried on across the bay and I could just make out the one bald patch amidst a forest of chest-high tea trees. Bill hovered the machine just long enough for Keith to jump out and get in position. This then meant that I could be filmed struggling to launch myself out of the helicopter.

We lifted off again for a flyby of the stack itself. In an instant we went from being ten feet above the forest to 400 feet above crashing waves battering against cliffs. This peninsula is like a piece of cheese. In the west it dips harmlessly into Fortescue Bay while in the east there are huge dizzying walls plunging menacingly into the Tasman Sea. Then there it was ... the Totem Pole. As a candle you would find on a child's birthday cake when viewed along side the real Candlestick, it didn't look impressive at all, like the runt of the litter among its giant family. No, from the air is not the ideal way to see the Tote. It hardly even looked real.

Richard and Keith were waiting for us when we came into hover. I had to wear a helmet 'to stop my head being cut off by the rotor blades' they said, and Brian was holding me on a leash like a pet dog. Jumping out of the helicopter wasn't as bad as I thought it was going to be. Having Richard right there in my face, asking me questions about what it was like seeing the tower again for the first time since my accident, however, was. How could I tell him that it didn't look very impressive at all? That wouldn't make very interesting TV, would it? I enthused. I lied.

It was about two kilometres from the landing site to the headland. Further than I had walked in the last year and then I would have to make it back again. The safety team had a stretcher on hand just in case I couldn't make it but I was determined. It was terrain that I wasn't used to, up and down steep hills and very rocky. If I had twisted an ankle, which was highly likely, that would be it, end of my story for the television. I could only just lift my leg over some boulders or fallen tree trunks and in one place I even had to traverse a crag. The slabby wall was about ten foot high with a shelf, just wide enough to take a foot, running horizontally across it. I had to negotiate that with a combination of hopping and one-armed slaps and at one point I very nearly overbalanced and fell backwards. Brian, Digger and John were clinging onto my ankles with arms held high like footballers gathered around the FA Cup, while I teetered on the brink.

When I arrived at the end of the promontory I peered over the cliff edge and saw the Totem Pole. The updraft was as if you put your head out of a car window travelling at sixty miles per hour. I felt joyous and alive for the first time in a year. I saw little beautiful things this time around that in my selfish rush to achieve I had never even noticed before: the lone eucalyptus tree at the very edge of the cliff, the huge logan stone poised dangerously on the angle, the pouf cushion plants clinging to the vertical walls of the Candlestick. The banksia trees with their unmistakable hairy cones like faces. And the lichen hanging like green Rasta's dreadlocks from all the tree branches. Apparently the presence of these lichens indicates the purity of the atmosphere hereabouts, which is undeniable.

And then there was the Pole itself. How could I not have noticed that single flowering plant growing out of the bare rock, right on top? How could I not have noticed that the top half was a completely different colour to the bottom half? Yes, the upper one hundred feet is lichen-covered and orangey-grey, whereas the lower hundred feet, up to the ledge where I lay for almost ten hours, is black and wave-polished. I imagined the waves that must on occasion run through the narrows. When the wind is coming from the west and blowing with certain ferocity and a swell is running, one can picture the scene. Half the tower submerged, white water coming right up to that ledge.

All my climbing life I've been dedicated to the pursuit of climbing such needles. Like a hunter of pointed trophies I have ascended towers from Pakistan to Patagonia, from the Arctic to the Equator, from the Utah Desert to the Himalaya. I suppose it is because there's no easy way up a tower, no path around the back. It is inaccessible without great skill and determination, on all sides. To quote the legend of pre-war climbing in Italy again, Comici has this to say:

> The climber who is able to divine the most logical and the most elegant way of reaching a summit, disdaining the easy slopes, and then follows that way, his nerves stretched to the limit, sensing his own inner conflict and aware of the effort needed to overcome the drag of the depths at his heels and the swirl of space around him ... That climber is creating a true work of art, sometimes of exceptional quality; a product of the spirit, an aesthetic sense of man, which will last for ever, carved on the rock walls, as long as the mountains themselves have life.

Perhaps I wanted to save big walks up snowy mountains for when I was older, but judging by how well I had just performed on the path, I allowed myself the indulgence of dreaming that I could, possibly, do them in a couple of years.

Watching Enga and Steve climbing the Totem Pole I had a sad, silent feeling, like a memory, but also those adrenaline surges that would not abate. I began to feel jealous as Steve climbed with fluid movements, Enga thoughtfully paying out the rope from her belay, hanging on a bolt. Enviously, I watched his move around arêtes and, with the grace of a primate, up a hand jam crack. Enga couldn't see him any more and she had to pay the rope out by feel alone, blind. I observed quietly as he smoothly surmounted my ledge and for an instant, as if in a freeze frame, with feet and hands on the ledge, I had the impression of an ape more than ever.

He slipped a keyhole hanger over the carrot and roared, to reach above the noise of the sea and round the stack to his rope mate,

'OK, ENGA. I'M SAFE. TAKE – OFF – BELAY.' As Steve was taking in the slack the rope whipped about in the gale and I was joined in my viewing by a sea lion who was watching so intently it might have been taking lessons in rope work. Enga had been hanging in her harness for two hours by this time and, although stiff with cold, made a fine job of climbing after Steve. He was sitting with his legs dangling over the side of the ledge and, playfully, she fell upon him when she got there. For a moment, so brief, I saw Celia and myself down there on that same ledge having a laugh.

It was now Enga's turn to lead on the top arête and I gave myself some slack in the safety rope the team had put there for my benefit to get a better view. She stood on the ledge with her head bowed, the fingers of each hand touching, like a gymnast contemplating, about to commence her routine. Then she launched off up the edge with all the strength of a power lifter and the nimbleness of a ballet dancer. After clipping the rope into the first bolt she paused and groped blindly with her right hand to find the side-pull, which would enable further upward progress. Second bolt . . . Third bolt . . . One can divide a climb of this type up into the sections between each bolt, a bit like a dot to dot drawing. The rock was damp from recent rain and the wind was still gusting with a gale's force.

I could see her swinging like a barn door every time a new gust of wind came forcing its way through the channel. John, who was in charge of making me safe, said in mild-mannered amazement, 'That channel's the perfect shape for measuring the Venturi Effect! And the Totem Pole is smack bang in the middle of it.' I could make out the grimace on her face, even though I was a hundred yards away, as she fought to stay in contact with the rock. Enga was slowing down, fatigue was taking her, but she was still making upward progress. Clinging on still. Fourth bolt . . . Then, like a dandelion head being blown on by a child – one o'clock, two o'clock, three o'clock, four – she parted company with the rock. For a brief moment the dandelion clock stood still and Enga was neither in contact with the rock nor in the act of falling. She was frozen in time and space, before the invisible thread that was suspending her broke and she plummeted, only a short fall. Enga lowered back down to the ledge dejected. I got the impression she had her heart set on this ascent. The wind and damp conditions and the stress of being filmed, and not being able to wait for calmer weather, had thwarted her.

Now Steve would try. He pulled the ropes through the karabiners and they swapped the ends around. Enga put the rope leading to him through the belay plate. I craned my neck over the cliff edge in the furious updraught but I couldn't see the rock scar from such a distance. I would have to wait for that until I could get a boat out, which we had planned for later. Steve's style of climbing was markedly different to Enga's. If Enga was a ballet dancer Steve was a boxer, hopping and prancing and snatching at hand holds. A skinny Mohamed Ali dancing and stinging. He paused where Enga had fallen and, obviously struggling, wiped the dampness off his hands onto his trouser leg. Then, reaching into the depths of his chalk bag with his right hand, he pulled out a small handful of the white powder to finish off the drying process. One's hands must be totally dry to climb well, as must be one's boot soles, which he kept wiping on the inside of his calf muscles in a kind of Irish jig.

Steve hung there, feet scrabbling, searching for a foot hold, almost off . . . Then he found one, a tiny rugosity and his feet stopped pedalling. If it wasn't for the gale you would have heard the producers, cameraman and safety crew breathe a sigh of relief. He regained his composure and clipped the rope into the fifth bolt. After resting on one toe for a couple of minutes he moved on up the arête with his customary ease. I could tell he was familiar with the climb when he reached up for a hand hold without even looking for its position. A good climber will always remember every important hold on a climb and that could be literally hundreds of holds. Now apply this to the thousands of routes Steve or Enga have done and that probably amounts to millions of holds all memorised and filed away for use at a later date. I considered this fact for a moment and then came to the conclusion that climbers are just plain weird.

He cruised up the final few feet and clambered onto the summit somewhat less stylishly than when he had set off on the climb. He was quite obviously knackered from his ascent. I now felt joy not jealousy at their success as Enga followed him up the last pitch. She trailed a rope behind her, which was attached to the top of the mainland cliff, the one they had abseiled on. This allowed them to rig up the all important rope traverse so as not to leave them stranded on top of the Totem Pole. Steve later told me that it was very strange for them, too, this returning to the Tote. They had kayaked out there and retrieved the rucsac a year ago. They had helped us all they could. Now, in a filming situation, the two of them felt at odds with their genuine feelings when acting in front of the camera.

The hour was getting late and I had to get back to the helicopter pickup site. With my entourage looking after me, and making sure I didn't slip on my slow walk back along the path, I felt very important. I could hear Meg's laugh, like a kookaburra, as she came trotting along the path behind us, her silver hair pasted to her forehead with sweat and spectacles askew.

Dave Cuthbertson enquired after my wellbeing in his Highland accent. I replied with a positive affirmation and spent the rest of the hour stumbling and falling and ruminating on his skill as a climber. Cubby was one of the best climbers in the world in the late 'eighties. Small, with the forearms of Popeye and a braveness to match, he is immensely strong and at the same time a mild-mannered gentleman. The first time I had seen him he was on the famous Snell's Field Boulder in Chamonix doing all sorts of gymnastic contortions without using his feet. He didn't have any use for such things as feet. I was sixteen years old at the time and very shy with it and didn't dare approach him.

Although I felt exhausted I made the return journey without any assistance. This was very important to me, as it is to any pilgrim. For that is what it was, a pilgrimage to pay my last respects to a lump of rock that had done me such damage. My journey had to be difficult and treacherous and scary for it to have any import, and it fulfilled my expectations admirably. I astonished myself how well I coped on this journey I was making, purely for sentimental reasons, to a sacred place. Forever onwards this place would be full of meaning for me, like hallowed ground. But I still had two more journeys to make; one to the Royal Hobart to visit all those nurses and therapists who brought me back into the land of the living, the other to see the rock scar that I hadn't been able to see from the cliff top.

I had a vivid and fevered dream that night in which I was climbing perfectly, high above the ocean. It could have been on any cliff but perhaps it was the Totem Pole. Anyway I was simply ascending without the least modicum of effort, occasionally using only the one finger of each hand, sitting my bum on my heels whilst dipping into my chalk bag. It was so realistic I could feel the wind in my hair, smell the sweetness of the salt and the ammonia of the bird shit upon the rock. It was seeing Enga and Steve climbing up that rock that did it, stirred in me passions for climbing that I wanted to forget about but, alas, they weren't very well buried.

Walking into the Royal Hobart Hospital I had the strangest feeling, that I was entering a grand museum or gallery because of the all-pervading echoing silence and the muted voices, which sounded like summer bumble-bees. I walked through the same door, took the same lift and walked down the same mile-long corridor, pausing only to study the picture of the child burn victim, still smiling. Stepping into reception of the Neuorological High Dependency Unit, I felt the adrenaline surge like I'd never felt on any rock climb. My gait went all to pot, stiff-legged and tiptoed with my arm raised up out to the side and bent, as if carrying an invisible bag of groceries.

Before, I hadn't noticed how little natural light there was in the reception area, only fluorescent lightbulbs, which cast a permanent twilight over the scene. Nurses I could recognise but whose names I couldn't remember gazed on me in amazement. I felt like some kind of Lazarus man, back from the dead. 'Lazarus, arise,' said the therapists, nurses and doctors of the Royal Hobart and so I did. But, unlike Lazarus whose return to life took only a day, my return took a whole year. I had no qualms about asking a person's name on which to hang their features, so it was with no trouble that I enquired the name of the woman with the familiar face and blonde hair who was always smiling. 'Andrea,' she said with a half grin, half laugh. 'You're coming on, aren't you? There's someone else who should be very pleased to see you. I'll just get her.' She ambled off into the darkness of a ward which was reserved for patients with photosensitive eyes.

Jane Boucher was the nurse I first wanted to see. We hugged. She had been expecting my arrival but not so soon. Jane was as full of youthful energy as I remembered, all big eyes, pale green and full lips with a strong body belying gentleness and compassion. We arranged to meet up for a coffee in Salamanca. She said in her sweet Tassie cadence that she couldn't chat now, 'Some people have work to do.' I told her that I understood and took myself off to see whom else I recognised.

There was Ian and Alison and Denny and Dr Mujic, Kylie and Jenny and Moy . . . Moy of whom I had been so terrified! She was tiny, I towered above her now that I was on my own two feet, but she was still stocky. I stared at her, not believing how I could have been so scared of her, so deluded. And as I stared, Nurse Moy walked over my grave and I remembered back to that time in ICU as if it was yesterday. The child in the cupboard, the six Jews, the roses, the old woman, and Nurse Moy giving the lethal injection. And now as she looked up at me, with a beaming smile, saying 'I read your book,' in her awkward Hoken Chinese accent, my fear of a woman, that I had been harbouring somewhere at the back of my injured brain for a year, melted away and I knew I could lay that nightmare of my past behind me.

*　　*　　*

Some deeply buried memories were brought back during my visit to Sue Duff, in her new wooden house built on stilts, some traumatic, some pleasant. There, in the doorway, was exactly the woman I recalled – mature and beautiful for it, with tied-back fiery red hair. To see me walking down her steep driveway she described as 'A miracle. I mean, when I last saw you you were on your back and now, after a year, you come strolling down my drive.' Sue asked me, in her northern English-cum-Tasmanian lilt, 'D'you find that you're getting any more spiritual these days?'

And I replied that I know that I should be and it must seem that, after three major accidents and not copping it, somebody somewhere is looking out for me. But my rational brain keeps telling me that it's all horrific coincidence. We spent our time reminiscing over what had come to pass in the last year. She said that I'd been given an amazing challenge and had risen to it.

We played around with plans to take disabled people trekking in Tibet, especially around Mount Kailas, a sacred mountain. It is said that one circumambulation erases the sins of a lifetime and heals all ills. We'll have to wait and see whether anything comes of it.

Sue was easy to talk to, so relaxed and disarming. I remember telling her something that I had never told anyone else before. I recounted to her how our safety man John Whittle had been listening to the radio and had heard on the news of an avalanche in his home town of Chamonix in which twelve people had died. He immediately telephoned Cham where he learnt that there was no damage to his house but that the gendarmes still hadn't released the names of his dead neighbours. He discovered at the same time that a young man called Jamie Fisher had died on the Droite's North Face. 'Did you know him?' he asked.

I had a clear picture of Jamie's face as he approached me in the Vaynol Arms, a local pub. He had a baby's face. 'Hell, he was only twenty-two,' I related to Sue. 'He was looking for information on a mountain called Meru in the Garhwal Himalaya.'

'I know it,' said Sue.

'I had attempted it and told him all I knew, especially about the approach gully, which was really very prone to avalanche. He had those eyes, extreme eyes. I remember worrying when he left for Meru thinking they'll either climb the mother or die. Luckily they all came home.'

I didn't know Jamie that well. In fact that night in the pub was the only night we'd met, but somehow his death, frozen on a ledge close to the top of the Droites, touched me. Looking at him that evening in the pub was like looking in a mirror, seeing the same obsession and single-mindedness that I displayed. Perhaps I was going that way? 'Let's just say that this accident might have saved my life. I was taking too many risks, pulling too much rope out of the bag.' I went on, 'It took something this serious, this close to the edge to stop me. And now I have been forced to stop I don't know what to do with myself.'

The date was Saturday, the 13th February, exactly one year to the day since my accident, the Totem Pole and my paper anniversary. The date on which I was joined to that piece of rock by phenomenal yet painful ceremony. I had come to see the rock scar, that ineffable space that was my undoing.

Rod Staples, whom we had met briefly last trip, came with his motor boat on a trailer behind his four by four. We met him at the Fox and Hounds and bumped and ground down the forestry road to Fortescue Bay. We put into the still water of the bay amidst stair-rod rain and motored off into the clagg. Up ahead the velveteen surface of the bay was punctured by this downpour, whilst behind it was churned up by the deafening double outboards. Rod had to put the propellers into reverse occasionally to shed them of kelp.

Our pilot told me of how he had come into the hospital two days after the accident had happened. As I was unconscious still, he just stood there quietly at the bedside. So I didn't see those piercing green eyes, the slightly buck teeth and the beard, slowly turning to grey.

The Candlestick was shoring up the cloud base as if it was a ceiling in danger of collapse, as a Doric column braces a Greek temple. There was then a thin layer of wispy fog creeping round the sides of the boat and muffling the engines. Sandwiched between this was a bleak panorama of wet gum forest and dark cliff with Pacific gulls showing us how clever they were. We motored by the Totem Pole and I was gutted to find that this, a larger boat than the one that rescued me, couldn't fit through the narrow channel. Was I to be thwarted at the last hurdle? Then Rod, sensing my dismay, said, 'We could still git in there from the other side. Don't give up hope just yit.' He cruised out past the Candlestick and steered to the east between the island at the very end of the peninsula and the Hippolytes, a group of islands well off shore but of the same igneous intrusion as the Tote. We were now on the opposite side of the headland, the wrong side to be able to see the rock scar but at least we had an excellent view of the tower. It felt as if we were in open sea now with a swell running and the wind getting up, the rain had soaked through our clothes long ago.

There was a very narrow cleft between the island and the Candlestick. This fissure was about ten feet wide and the side walls were upwards of 330 feet high. If we could get through there we would be rewarded with a view of the whole Tote from the west but, more than that, perhaps a sight of the rock scar. Richard and Keith were keen to give it a try as they could film my reaction.

'Why don't we go for it,' said Rod, surprising himself perhaps more than us. 'If I reverse in there we cin zoom out if we git into deep shit.'

There was an eight-foot swell running through that gap and, as we went in there, backwards, I couldn't shake the impression of the Symplegades, the clashing rocks of Greek heroic legend. I was one of the Argonauts on the voyage to Colchis. It was a crazy stunt to pull but I felt exhilarated and excited at my imminent meeting with my 'maker' (in my present body).

As we entered the clashing rocks the swell threw us around like

192

a toy and it was with great skill that Rod avoided running the boat into the cliffs. Then, suddenly, there it was, pencil-thin and towering above the boat. One didn't need a magnifying glass to see the scar. It was dead obvious, about eighty feet up and on the left edge of a slanting crack. I thought it was going to be the size of a house brick. Steve and Enga had told me so, but the scar they had been looking at was on the opposite side of the Pole. The scar I was now seeing you could slot a television set into, a portable admittedly, but still huge. I was experiencing deep shock. How did that thing not kill me? It must have been travelling at the very least seventy miles an hour when it struck me! How did I avoid quadriplegia? A rock that size could have easily broken my neck. It's no surprise that I had whiplash for two whole months. I felt humbled and just happy to be alive.

Rod asked, 'Have you seen enough yit?' I replied that I had and he said, 'Good, thin, lit's git the hill outta here.' He revved up the outboards and sped off, bringing the boat perilously close to the side wall of the Candlestick.

Once out in the open ocean, chilled and wet through, I couldn't shake a grin off my face. As we motored in a westerly direction back past the Hippolytes I was thrilled to have executed my plan, finished my journey.

The torrent had subsided now and eased to sporadic spluttering showers that dripped off the plastic canopy of the boat. Back in the bay the water was glassy smooth, the ceiling of cloud had lifted to 600 feet and was a grey blanket covering the whole world, as far as we knew. The mist had dissipated off the sea. Amidst the roar of the outboards I looked left to see the Tote in all its glory, standing proud and erect and ankle deep in salty water. As we passed it by I was forced to twist my head ever backwards if I was to keep my eyes on it until the last. For I knew that this would be the final time we would meet.

This tower had been inextricably linked to my life for exactly a year now. There wasn't a day went by when I did not think about, analyse, dismantle or downright curse the day that I ever heard of the Totem Pole. But now I saw it for what it was, the most slender and, dare I say it, beautiful sea stack on the planet. I held no animosity towards it. How can you hold a grudge against an inanimate object? A piece of rock! For God's sake that's all it was.

I gazed on as the Totem Pole slowly disappeared behind Cape Hauy and, as I sat shivering in my wet clothes, there was only warmth in my heart. I could only appreciate the top quarter of a stack now and, as I wound my head around even further, I could just make out its eccentric angles in the flat light. And when it was finally dissolved from view I found that I had broken into a broad smile within and without.

10

TASMANIAN REFLECTIONS

Sometimes difficulty is the greatest friend of the soul.

John O'Donohue,
Anam Cara

'Guess what? Enga got to lead the Totem Pole.' Steve gabbled in his excitement to give me the news and so failed to give me the opportunity of guessing. 'Yeah, she freed it all the way.' He now had a huge beam on his face as if to say, 'Go on ask me, ask me!' So, sipping my flat black, I questioned him as to what else he had done. 'Only free climbed the first pitch of the Murcian route up the Pole.' I didn't really understand where the Murcian route began and so asked him where it started.

'Where does it start? Where does it start? It just follows the crack that the block came from that spannered you in the head, that's all!'

Pete Steane was at the cafe with us and he knew exactly where the route lay.

'Did you drill many carrots in it?'

'Just three,' replied Steve.

Pete nodded silently. He hadn't changed, just as cool as ever.

'There was a ton of loose rock in there. Really weird for a wave blasted obelisk such as that. You actually use the rock scar as a hand hold now!'

'How hard is it?' asked Pete.

'Easier than the original free route. That's the amazing thing about it. I mean why did I not look there when I did the first free ascent?' Steve shook his head, giggling.

There was something familiar about the music that was wafting over on the breeze to the tables outside the cafe. It took me a moment to place 'El Condor Pasa', and then I was transported back to the Salamanca of a year ago. It was the very same Peruvian pan pipe band that had played at the Saturday market twelve months since. All of a sudden Celia was there pushing me through the heaving throng of people, me staring at a mass of arses and bollocks. Myrtle bowls exquisitely turned, fiddleback Huon pine boxes, pepper mills, picture frames and spoons of sassafras, genuine Australian hats, jewellery and tasty food. All this stuff meant nothing to me then as I passed by a thousand crotches. Now I could rejoice with the many hippies in the park, saunter around perusing each stallholder's wares, tasting the free samples.

Leaving the table I went in search of the pipe band just so I could throw a dollar into the felt-lined guitar case, like I did a year ago. I wanted to shout to them there and then, over the sound of the music, 'DO YOU REMEMBER ME? THE GUY IN THE WHEELCHAIR FROM A YEAR AGO? THE ONE WITH A BALD HEAD? THE CRIPPLE? WELL, LOOK AT ME NOW! I'M WALKING! I'M WALKING!' But I luckily restrained myself.

I had never noticed so many hemiplegics before I had become one. At the Saturday market I saw one after another, most of them stallholders. Now that I was one I could instantly spy the telltale signs, the weak leg, the crooked arm, the slack arm. Most of them were moving on through the years and I guessed that their lives had been altered by strokes. There was the man dismantling the stall, removing the high crossbars by thrusting a specially developed pole upwards and tapping it, with amazing accuracy, onto the beams – like tossing the caber with one hand. Or the other bloke who was pinching heavy planks between the fingers and thumb of his one usable hand and loading them into a trailer. I could have said that they were suffering from the effects of a stroke, but I would be wrong. They aren't suffering any more. I'm not suffering any more. We have had our lives altered. We are just different.

Steve and I exchanged hugs and Pete and I left the table and walked across the street to his car. We must have looked a right sight, the two of us, him with his callipers and limbo walk and me with my stick and leg flying out to the right. All eyes were upon us and I said to Pete, 'I don't know about you but I feel like a rock star.' We were getting more attention than I'd ever had and I felt somehow special. 'You'll get used to that,' he replied.

The following night I arranged to meet Dawn and Nicola, my two physiotherapists, in a North Hobart bar. Jane Boucher and I went up there together and arrived before them. It was a crowded Irish theme pub just like every city has.

'Do you remember the very first sentence you strung together?' asked Nick, barely able to hold back a full belly laugh. 'It was "I'm dyin' for a dump,"' she said, mocking my broad Lancashire accent with a stand up comic's ease. 'We all cracked up.'

Dawn gave me a wallet of photographs which she had taken the previous year of the team and me in the physio gym. I was touched and horrified at the same time. Touched that she had thought of me and horrified to see myself and the state I was in. I hadn't seen photos of me a year ago and had forgotten just how ill I looked, gaunt with a skinhead, and skeletal. There was the one picture where I had both hands on a big gym ball, Nick supporting my right side, the scar clearly visible in my skull and I was trying to force a smile, drooping radically on the one side. It was as though a shadow had been removed and I perceived just how far I had travelled along the road of recovery.

The days all seem to blend into one another when I look back but one day, about lunchtime, Jane packed an old rusting blue Datsun saloon with enough food for three days, plus camping gear. We then took off for a three-hour drive to the Freycinet Peninsula on the east coast of Tasmania.

'I want to show you one of my special places,' Jane said. 'It's called Wineglass Bay for obvious reasons. You'll see why when you get there.'

Motoring past a stretch of rocky coastline, I made the mistake of asking how far the walk to this Wineglass Bay actually was.

'Only three or four miles.'

I became seriously worried about my ability to walk four miles and very suspicious at the same moment. We drifted slowly past vineyards and along a coast arched with deserted white beaches.

'Look, there it is, the Freycinet.'

There in the distance, framed by the sun, was a mountainous peninsula with the thin white threads of breaking waves along its whole length.

We arrived at a car park in the late 'arvo' and set off walking almost immediately in a race to beat dusk. I was determined to walk over the Hazards, a bare granite mountain range rising straight up out of the ocean, in one push. It was the first time I'd worn a rucsac to walk further than the shops and it kept threatening to overbalance me, though Jane carried the bulk of the equipment.

'I feel like a back seat bush walker,' Jane said, 'every time I see you stumble I want to tell you where to put your foot.'

I had the feeling that I was performing graded moves on rock, bouldering, when in fact I was just staggering along a path, so heavy did my legs feel and so awkward were the uneven rocks under my feet. Giant and golden potato boulders lined the path and, as I passed them by, I fingered holes and felt edges, a subconscious habit that was proving hard to break. How I longed to climb upon them.

Harbingers of doom in the guise of innocent tourists came down the path towards us.

'It's a hell of a way,' said one red faced, overweight, middle-aged fellow.

Another, even bigger and gasping for his breath, told me, 'I don't fancy your chances, mate.'

I turned around astonished and said, 'Thanks for the vote of confidence.'

Coming over the pass between Mount Amos and Mount Mayson was a very emotional moment. If I could achieve this in one year, nature only knows what I could achieve in two years or three. 'Bloody hell, I can do anything I want to now,' I said, amazed at my performance. Jane gave me a congratulatory peck on the cheek. I now knew that I would be able to go walking in my beloved hills, something which had been so doubtful for the last twelve months. I know of treks in the Himalayas, long treks, pilgrim trails that have been worn flat by thousands upon thousands of feet marching through time, that I could hike now. I choked up and a tear welled in my eye.

'I reckon this is a moment you should have to yourself, I'll leave you to your thoughts,' Jane offered. But I said that I could imagine no better company.

A little later she said, 'Now you see why it's called Wineglass Bay.'

It was a complete, perfect wineglass, the mouth being narrower than the bowl, which was trimmed with a bow of brilliant white sand. It seemed to take forever to stumble down the lee of the mountain to that beach and, in my state of fatigue, I slowly became aware that the forest had taken on a glowing, preternatural greenness. This I had only felt at times of extreme exhaustion, when descending out of the mountains on the Baffin Island trip, or having spent twenty-one days on a vertical wall on the Central Tower of Paine, starved of colour except for the grey of new granite and the white of snow. Colours then take on a vividness which one wishes one could see throughout the whole of one's life. I fell on the path many times, sometimes without injury, sometimes with injury and so finally towed my spent body onto the beach.

Curious pademelons hopped down out of the foliage as Jane set up camp and cooked dinner. I felt feeble and emasculated. I tried to put the hoop tent up with one arm but you certainly need two arms to do that (some reckon two people). A storm was brewing and at one point the tent blew away down the beach in the grey twilight in the rain. I was reduced to a spectator as Jane ran about attempting to seize the cursed thing. Instead I tottered around, searching for rocks to hold the flysheet down in the soft sand. Eventually I was ordered into the small tent under threat of no dinner. I complied and a rich meal of rehydrated broccoli, courgettes and noodles was delivered forthwith. Through the tent's entrance I couldn't see the bald skulls of Mount Parson and Mount Dove any more, they had their heads in the clouds.

I had spent months in tents in base camps around the world. But this was the first night I had spent under canvas for over a year and, with the rain pelting down and the wind blowing strong, it felt a joy to be back.

At the Retro Cafe in Salamanca I met Neale Smith, my paramedic rescuer. He was supposed to be interviewed for the television but had been taking a holiday in Fiji during the week of filming. We sat down at an outside table under an umbrella and drank a couple of cold Boags. His voice was so soft and kindly that it took me straight back to the accident – 'You'll be all right, cobber.' I said what a shame it was that he wasn't interviewed and he replied, 'That's too bad. I could have been a film star.'

Now was the first time that I got the story of my rescue at first hand, from a source other than that which my tormented mind had created. For all I knew this could have been completely fictitious, a bizarre construct of my imagination.

Neale began, 'We couldn't get near you in the chopper and the pilot had to put it down a couple of kliks away. Paul Steane and I hurried to you, not knowing what to expect.'

Meanwhile, Tom Jamieson had been sitting by me on that shelf, shivering in his impotence, for six hours, when Neale dropped in on the end of the rope.

'Blood had puddled to a depth of two millimetres all over the ledge,' grimaced Neale, 'and I was worried about moving your spine but I figured that if Celia had already hauled you up, then any damage that could have been done had been done already. I put a surgical collar on you just in case.' I sat transfixed, ignoring my bottle of beer as he went on. 'I had to be fairly rough with you to get you clipped onto my helicopter harness and then, in the gathering gloom, we went over the side. You were like a sack of spuds with stigmata. Anyway, although the boat pilot was doing his best to keep her steady we missed the tinny on the first attempt and nearly ended up in the drink.' He took a sip from his bottle and so did I. Then he continued, 'On the second attempt I threw the end of the rope, which was dangling in the water, to the guys. They pulled me, with you attached, and I hooked my legs into the tinny for dear life. All that was left for them to do was to pull you in.'

I was shocked. I thought he'd been there by my side for hours and it turned out that the whole operation, once he had reached me, took only twenty minutes.

'Once in the tub we had to get out between the Candlestick and the island,' he told me. For some reason I imagined that we'd escaped to the Fortescue Bay side (the route we had taken with the Boy Racer) but the seventeen-foot tinny wouldn't fit through such a narrow gap, so we had taken the Clashing Rocks route we'd done with the film crew.

We paid up, left a dollar for the waitress, and drove up to Mount Nelson Semaphore Station. There, in the nineteenth century the keeper used to receive signals from Port Arthur penal institution, over one hundred kilometres distant, warning of escaped convicts. We sat on a bench overlooking the city with its huge natural harbour. Neale pointed out over the estuary to where he lived while the sun beat down with an intensity I hadn't felt before. There was a cruise ship clearly visible down in the port and the white-haired cruisers were climbing down off a coach into the car park of the Semaphore Station. They each had a large badge on their lapels with a name on it and we joked that if they forgot who they were they would only have to look down at their chests.

★　　★　　★

During the long flight home, in the dark of the night's cabin I lay awake, wide awake, motionless. With the griping of babies and the snoring of old men, all I could think about was the rugged coastline of Tasmania and how it knocked me into a new life. New adventures would be mine for the taking but I would have to be patient, a couple more years they tell me, before I can realise them. Two more years of brain plasticity in which to plan my escapades.

11

CELIA'S STORY

The best part of a year had gone by since Celia and I had seen each other. Sailing around the Falklands, South Georgia and Antarctica was how she had spent the last six months. After my return from Tasmania Celia came round to my little house in Llanberis. When I answered that familiar knock on the door we played off each other, two positively charged particles, not knowing how to treat one another. But that feeling wore off after just a few minutes and we were back to being the good friends we always should have been. I told her about Neale's account of the accident and begged her to fill in the last blank spots in my story.

'I remember the effort, the sheer physical effort of making that rope move the barest of fractions. I remember my incredulity at eventually achieving such a laborious task. I remember the deep wounds in my hands from pulling so frantically on the rope. I remember my back hurting like hell where the harness dug deep, bruising my waist. I know there are ways I could have done it faster, but this way was ingrained. I knew it worked as long as I had the brute strength in me.'

After a while she said, 'How differently you and I must view that day. Did you recall the time passing?' I shook my head. Celia continued, 'I had to forget about minutes and just function. It gave me strength being capable of functioning under that pressure. I think I've forgotten how much I hated it.'

I asked her what else she remembered of the rescue.

'I'm running and running, feet in sandals slapping the red earth, flashing beetle green. Running round rocks, leaping logs and brushing branches, running and breathing. I remember repeating like a mantra, "Running saves lives – breathe – running saves lives – breathe – running saves lives".

'Somewhere behind me you were lying on a ledge halfway up the Totem Pole. I didn't know if you were bleeding to death. Had you slipped into unconsciousness? Had you fallen off the ledge and were now hanging helpless? Were still alive? I had to stop thinking! Stop panicking. Just run and breathe.

'I was maybe halfway there when I met these two Aussie climbers. I must have looked a right state with blood all over me. I babbled at them "There's been an accident. There's a guy badly injured on the Totem Pole." I sent one of them to be near you but told him no way to cross the Tyrolean. I told the other one to come with me but he couldn't keep up with me. So I asked him to go back to his mate because I couldn't get the image out of my mind of that one guy trying to cross the Tyrolean and falling to his death. I had no idea how experienced they were. They could have been complete beginners for all I knew.'

These facts sent a wave of shivers down my spine. I was lucky that they disregarded Celia's order.

'It must have been between four and five in the afternoon now. I couldn't believe it was Friday the 13th. How could this day turn into this nightmare? I had blood on my hands, blood under my fingernails, red and crusty, blood streaked with sweat across my face and neck. Not my blood, your blood.'

I asked her about the actual technicalities of the rescue, the nuts and bolts, but she was hesitant, reluctant even, to discuss such trivialities with me. She would just say that any experienced mountaineer could effect such a rescue, preferring instead, to tell me how she felt on that awful day. So I left her to say what she felt, and she started at the beginning.

'A black square of rock.' She halted, seemingly confused by the English language. 'A bolt, a rusty peg.' Another long pause. 'Wire and karabiners, ropes tied in knots equalising the pull of the downward rope . . .' Again she stopped and I was hanging on her words . . . 'That you now climbed up from your sea-washed platform. I remember a pillar just too wide to bear-hug. There was too much swell to climb the lower pitch and, to tell the truth, I was relieved. You were jumaring up the rope to this ledge where I crouched, perfecting the belay. I wasn't happy on that ledge. The Tyrolean onto that straw of rock, the abseil down to the ledge and the climbing ahead of me, that place made me nervous. I made you nervous, too. Do you remember telling me that I was freaking you out? They were the last normal words you said as you abseiled away from me.'

I sat, with moist eyes, feeling remorseful for the misery I had put everybody I loved through. I said simply, 'Sorry.'

Celia responded, 'Someone said when we were at Hobart Hospital that good would come out of all this misery and pain. They were right. The experience of the accident, your recovery, your will, determination and achievement . . . some memories so painful and yet I feel like I'm living life like never before. What was it that poet wrote? "Catch the joy as it flies by"?

'Then came the shouting to come down to the ledge, fix the rope, so that you could climb up and we could climb the top pitch. So down I slithered, breathing carefully. I set up a belay with many anchors. "OK, it's all ready for you to jumar up," I yelled. I concentrated on that belay, watching it closely as you weighted the rope, the responsibility of your safety weighing on my conscience. This was my last view of normality.'

With some effort I rose from my armchair and fell into the kitchen to make us a brew before returning to the bad dream, transfixed.

'And then it was shattered. The ugly tear and crash of a rock. I remember fear grabbing me. I shook it off and thought, no, it's not possible! Normality left me, sitting in that dark corner wretchedly observing those textbook knots. I had to pull my gaze away from the black rock and I stared down shouting, "Paul, Paul!"'

Afterwards, she told me, she wrote things down. She passed me a beaten up exercise book with some scribblings in it. If I didn't know her writing so well I would have had trouble reading it:

'He is there beneath me, hung by a thread of fate and nylon. He is suspended navel up ... Limbs thrown out. He is limp and lifeless, faded. Here are the dying petals of a once exuberant flower. Just beyond, the sea is drinking thirstily at his blood. Horror is roaring in my ears. These tentacles of seaweed, they're unfurling, they're stroking softly as the sacrificial red, beckoning him to join them in their sempiternal kingdom.'

At the same time she had to focus on the job in hand. 'Breathe, girl, breathe, I thought. Think. Think. I must be safe. If I fuck up now, that's it. We're both going to go. Tie in the rope. One time, two times, three times. I had to be safe. For all I knew you were dying down there. I was scared.'

It was self-evident by the way Celia was talking that she had to get things off her chest, too. It was as much a catharsis for her as it was for me.

She continued, 'I shouted again to you, "Paul, Paul – can you hear me? I'm coming down. I'll be with you soon. I won't be long, darling." Then I noticed the rope and I thought, fucking thing! I knew it would get tangled. I didn't need this. I remember thinking, Oh, come on. Slow down. Breathe.

'I remember the look on your face when I reached you. Eyes saying everything, I clasped your hand, exchanging hope ... and energy. I talked at you, assuming you knew where you were. Then you croaked, "What's happened?" and so I got you upright in an arrangement of slings and put my helmet on you. Then I jumared back to the ledge and set up a Yosemite haul. The rest you know ... apart from the drive!'

'Tell me about the drive.'

'I watched the helicopter rise steeply, zooming off towards Hobart Hospital. It was ten in the evening and at last you were off to safety. I could slump back and relinquish my responsibility. Despite the rescue team's efforts I had felt on standby, knowing I could still act if they failed. The ambulance team called it shock and protected me from what they called my superwoman persona. Now I wanted the hot drink and blanket, the arm around my shoulder.

'But you were 100 kilometres away by now and I was in the wrong place. I had to get to you. They let me go, their responsibility finished, too. It wasn't over for me though. It was only just beginning. I set off along dirt trails through the forest. Faster, faster. I just stared blankly through the windshield. I had to keep checking the speed, as I was unsure of my judgement. Not too fast . . . and keep awake. I turned on the radio but all the stations were playing Heavy Metal. Black Sabbath was churning out "Heaven n' Hell'. Friday the 13th, you see. The miles drifted by in a daze, until "Welcome to Hobart" a sign said. But I was dreading this moment . . . the reception desk at Accident and Emergency, open a door and there you were. Alive!'

She paused and, with tears in her eyes, finished her story.

'"Paul," I whispered, holding your hand. We made eye contact. You forced me an imperceptible smile that only I could recognise. A pool of thick scarlet blood had collected on the floor beneath your head. Dripping off the end of the stretcher. Red . . . for Valentine's Day.'

After I had heard Celia out I knew I had laid my ghosts to rest. Though Tasmania hurt me so badly I have found curious atonement in writing this story down. It is catharsis like I have never felt before. With my last two accidents I had no repressed experiences but here, with the head injury, I had; namely the gruesome nightmare of the accident, my terrifying days in intensive care and the emotive parting with Celia. The only way to purge these events was to think about them for a year solidly, and that is what I have done. Every waking moment, and quite a few sleeping moments, have been spent thinking, studying and reworking the accident and its aftermath. Now it is time to move on. To forget, but yet learn from what is past, and has passed, as well as I am able and find a new way of living.

I have seen things with new eyes since my accident, especially the relative importance of acts such as climbing rocks, acts that I once thought I would rather die than do without. For mountains and rocks don't care whether you climb them or not. Driving in the taxi past Llanfairfechan, with the man who put his hand into a nest of snakes, I was overjoyed to note that there on the central reservation was the same sight I had seen a year previously – ablaze, thousands of profound yellow as yolk daffodils, their bulbs invisible, deep in the dark Welsh earth.

The germ of a new life.